India's Foreign Policy and Diplomacy

Emerging Scenario and Challenges

India's Foreign Policy and Diplomacy

Emerging Scenario and Challenges

Edited by

C. Vinodan

Co-ordinator, Rajiv Gandhi Chair for Public Policy Studies
and
Honorary Director, Institute for Contemporary Chinese Studies (ICCS), School of International Relations and Politics, Mahatma Gandhi University, Kottayam, Kerala

New Century Publications
New Delhi, India

NEW CENTURY PUBLICATIONS
4800/24, Bharat Ram Road,
Ansari Road, Daryaganj,
New Delhi - 110 002 (India)

Tel.: 011-2324 7798, 4358 7398, 6539 6605
Fax: 011-4101 7798
E-mail: indiatax@vsnl.com • info@newcenturypublications.com
www.newcenturypublications.com

Editorial office:
LG–7, Aakarshan Bhawan,
4754-57/23, Ansari Road, Daryaganj,
New Delhi – 110 002

Tel.: 011-4356 0919

First Published: **2017**

ISBN: **978-81-7708-436-8**

Published by New Century Publications and printed at Salasar Imaging Systems, New Delhi.

Designs: Patch Creative Unit, New Delhi.

PRINTED IN INDIA

About the Book

India has formal diplomatic relations with most countries of the world. India is a regional power, a nascent global power and a potential superpower. India has a growing international influence and a prominent voice in global affairs.

After India gained Independence from the United Kingdom in 1947, it strongly supported independence movements in other colonies. Jawaharlal Nehru, India's first Prime Minister, was the architect of India's foreign policy. During the Cold War, India adopted a foreign policy of not aligning itself with any major power bloc. However, India developed close ties with the Soviet Union and received extensive military support from it. The end of the Cold War significantly affected India's foreign policy, as it did for much of the world.

In the post-Cold War era, a significant aspect of India's foreign policy is the 'Look East Policy' launched in 1992. India's growing economy, strategic location, and a large and vibrant Diaspora have won it more allies and partners. India has friendly relations with several countries in the developing world. The foreign policy of Prime Minister Narendra Modi indicates a shift towards focusing on the Asian region and, more broadly, trade deals.

This volume contains 9 research articles, authored by scholars in the field of political science, international relations, comparative politics, economics, security studies, and political economy. These contributions provide useful material to understand contemporary dynamics of India's foreign policy and diplomacy.

About the Editor

Dr. C. Vinodan is currently Co-ordinator, Rajiv Gandhi Chair for Public Policy Studies and Honorary Director, Institute for Contemporary Chinese Studies (ICCS), School of International Relations and Politics, Mahatma Gandhi University, Kottayam, Kerala. He has worked previously at the Post-graduate and Research Department of Political Science, Sree Narayana College, Kollam and Department of Political Science, University of Kerala.

He obtained his M.A. (II Rank), M.Phil. and Ph.D. degrees in political science from the University of Kerala. He was awarded the Visiting Scholar Fellowship (2003) by the Claremont Graduate University, California, USA. He has attended numerous courses in international relations in India and abroad. These include the 2016 Sino-Indian Cross-Cultural Dialogues held by the Institute of Advanced International Studies, Sun Yat-sen University, Guangzhou, China; and the US Department of States Fulbright American Studies Institute (FASI) course on foreign policy at the University of Delaware, Philadelphia in 2000.

Dr. Vinodan has also attended and presented papers at various national and international conferences/seminars. He is also the recipient of a number of awards including the Kerala University Post-doctoral Award (2003-2005). He is also a member of the editorial board of the *Journal of Human Security; Indian Journal of Politics and International Relations* and *South Asian Journal of Diplomacy*. He has published 40 research papers and 4 books.

His areas of teaching and research activities include international relations, security studies, Chinese studies, South Asian studies, energy, environment and human security.

Contents

Contributors

Shibashis Chatterjee	Professor, Department of International Relations, Jadavpur University, Kolkata.
W. Lawrence S. Prabhakar	Associate Professor, Department of Political Science, Madras Christian College, Chennai.
Sanjay K. Jha	Professor and Dean, School of International Studies, Central University of Gujarat, Gandhinagar.
V. Suryanarayan	Formerly Professor and Director, Centre for South and South East Asian Studies, University of Madras, Chennai.
Pavithran K.S.	Professor and Head, Department of Political Science, Calicut University, Calicut.
Anurag Tripathi	Assistant Professor, Department of International Studies and History, Christ University, Bangalore.
B. Krishnamurthy	Professor, Department of Politics and International Studies, Pondicherry University, Puducherry.
Vijayata Rani	Research Scholar, Department of Politics and International Relations, Pondicherry University, Puducherry
Anu Unny	Assistant Professor, Department of Political Science, University of Kerala, Thiruvananthapuram.
Rajiv Bhatia	Distinguished Fellow at Gateway House, Mumbai; formerly, Director General, Indian Council of World Affairs (ICWA); Ambassador to several countries.

Preface

India, as an emerging global power, represents a vast spectrum of geo-political and geo-economic realities. The second largest country in demographic terms, India is one of the most diverse and pluralistic nations in the world having different languages, cultures, religions and social identities. Though it is an emerging economic power with an impressive record of economic growth in recent years, India still encounters some of the most serious problems such as poverty, unemployment, repression of women and underprivileged, and inequalities, both in terms of living conditions and access to educational and health facilities.

Globalization and a thriving domestic economy are changing the face of India rapidly. It ranks fourth (after US, Russia and China) in terms of military power in the world. India is considered as an emerging global power trying to assert its legitimate position in the evolving global system. India engages with the world vigorously and actively to further its national interests. No wonder, it has emerged as a force to be reckoned with in the global comity of nations. India is the largest democracy with vibrant democratic institutions and a liberal Constitution.

India has formal diplomatic relations with most countries of the world. India is a regional power, a nascent global power and a potential superpower.

India was one of the founding members of several international organisations including United Nations, Asian Development Bank (ADB), G-20 and the Non-Aligned Movement (NAM). It has also forged close ties with the member states of the Association of Southeast Asian Nations (ASEAN), the African Union, and the Arab League.

Jawaharlal Nehru, India's first Prime Minister, promoted a strong personal role for the Prime Minister but a weak institutional structure for foreign policy matters. Nehru served concurrently as Prime Minister and Minister of External Affairs.

He made all major foreign policy decisions himself after consulting his advisers and then entrusted the conduct of international affairs to senior members of the Indian Foreign Service. He was the main founding fathers of the *Panchsheel* or the five principles of peaceful co-existence.

After India gained Independence from the United Kingdom in 1947, it soon joined the Commonwealth of Nations and strongly supported independence movements in other colonies. During the Cold War, India adopted a foreign policy of not aligning itself with any major power bloc. However, India developed close ties with the Soviet Union and received extensive military support from it. The end of the Cold War significantly affected India's foreign policy, as it did for much of the world.

India's international influence varied over the years after Independence. Indian prestige and moral authority were high in the 1950s and facilitated the acquisition of developmental assistance from both East and the West. Although the prestige stemmed from India's non-aligned stance, the nation was unable to prevent Cold War politics from becoming intertwined with interstate relations in South Asia.

In the 1960s and 1970s, India's international position among developed and developing countries faded in the course of wars with China and Pakistan, disputes with other countries in South Asia, and India's attempt to balance Pakistan's support from the United States and China by signing the Indo-Soviet Treaty of Friendship and Cooperation in August 1971. Although India obtained substantial Soviet military and economic aid, which helped to strengthen the nation, India's influence was undercut regionally and internationally by the perception that its friendship with the Soviet Union prevented a more forthright condemnation of the Soviet presence in Afghanistan. In the late 1980s, India improved relations with the United States, other developed countries, and China while continuing close ties with the Soviet Union. Relations with its South Asian neighbours, especially Pakistan, Sri Lanka, and Nepal, occupied much of the energies of the Ministry of External Affairs.

Since the dissolution of the Soviet Union, India has forged a closer partnership with Western powers. In the 1990s, India's economic problems and the demise of the bipolar world political system forced India to reassess its foreign policy and adjust its foreign relations. Previous policies proved inadequate to cope with the serious domestic and international problems facing India. The end of the Cold War gutted the core meaning of non-alignment and left Indian foreign policy without significant direction. The hard, pragmatic considerations of the early 1990s were still viewed within the non-aligned framework of the past, but the disintegration of the Soviet Union removed much of India's international leverage, for which relations with Russia and the other post-Soviet states could not compensate. After the dissolution of the Soviet Union, India improved its relations with the United States, Canada, France, Japan and Germany. In 1992, India established formal diplomatic relations with Israel and this relationship has grown since then.

In the mid-1990s, India attracted the world attention towards the Pakistan-backed terrorism in Kashmir. The Kargil War resulted in a major diplomatic victory for India. The United States and European Union recognised the fact that Pakistani military had illegally infiltrated into Indian territory and pressured Pakistan to withdraw from Kargil. Several anti-India militant groups based in Pakistan were labelled as terrorist groups by the United States and the European Union.

In 1998, India tested nuclear weapons for the second time which resulted in several US, Japanese and European sanctions on India. India's then defence minister, George Fernandes, said that India's nuclear programme was necessary as it provided a deterrence to potential Chinese nuclear threat. Most of the sanctions imposed on India were removed by 2001.

After September 11 attacks in 2001, Indian intelligence agencies provided the US with significant information on Al-Qaeda and related groups' activities in Pakistan and Afghanistan. India's extensive contribution to the 'war on terror', coupled with a surge in its economy, has helped India's diplomatic relations with several countries.

In the post-Cold War era, a significant aspect of India's foreign policy is the 'Look East Policy'. During the Cold War, India's relations with its South East Asian neighbours were not very strong. After the end of the Cold War, the government of India realised the importance of redressing this imbalance in India's foreign policy. Consequently, in the early 1990s, the government of Prime Minister Narsimha Rao unveiled the 'Look East Policy'. Initially, it focused on renewing political and economic contacts with the countries of East and South-East Asia.

'Look East Policy' was launched in 1992 just after the end of the Cold War, following the dissolution of the Soviet Union. The policy was given an initial thrust with the then Prime Minister Narasimha Rao visiting China, Japan, South Korea, Vietnam and Singapore and India becoming an important dialogue partner with ASEAN in 1992. Since the beginning of this century, India has given a big push to this policy by becoming a summit level partner of ASEAN (2002) and getting involved in some regional initiatives such as the Bay of Bengal Initiative for Multi-Sectoral Technical and Economic Cooperation (BIMSTEC) and the Ganga-Mekong Co-operation. It became a member of the East Asia Summit (EAS) in December 2005.

India has been pushing for reforms in the UN and WTO with mixed results. India's candidature for a permanent seat at the UN Security Council is currently backed by several countries including France, Russia, the United Kingdom, Germany, Japan, Brazil, Australia and UAE. In 2004, the United States signed a nuclear co-operation agreement with India even though the latter is not a part of the Nuclear Non-Proliferation Treaty. The US argued that India's strong nuclear non-proliferation record made it an exception, however this has not persuaded other Nuclear Suppliers Group members to sign similar deals with India. India's growing economy, strategic location, mix of friendly and diplomatic foreign policy and large and vibrant Diaspora has won it more allies than enemies. India has friendly relations with several countries in the developing world.

Russia is the largest supplier of military equipment to India, followed by Israel and France. According to some analysts, Israel is set to overtake Russia as India's largest military and strategic partner. The two countries also collaborate extensively in the sphere of counter-terrorism and space technology. India also enjoys strong military relations with several other countries, including the United Kingdom, the United States, Japan, Singapore, Brazil, South Africa and Italy. In addition, India operates an airbase in Tajikistan, signed a landmark defence accord with Qatar in 2008, and has leased out Assumption Island from Seychelles to build a naval base in 2015.

India has also forged relationships with developing countries, especially South Africa, Brazil, and Mexico. These countries often represent the interests of the developing countries at various global economic forums such as World Trade Organization (WTO).

India's foreign policy has always regarded the concept of neighbourhood as one of widening concentric circles, around a central axis of historical and cultural commonalities.

As many as 21 million people of Indian origin live and work abroad and constitute an important link with the mother country. An important role of India's foreign policy has been to ensure their welfare and well-being within the framework of the laws of the country where they live.

The foreign policy of Prime Minister Narendra Modi indicates a shift towards focusing on the Asian region and, more broadly, trade deals.

I place on record my deep gratitude and appreciation for all the contributors to this volume for their respective scholarly articles which will surely add, constructively, to the existing body of literature on India's foreign policy and diplomacy.

Kottayam **C. Vinodan**

1

India's Foreign Policy in the Post-Cold War Era

Shibashis Chatterjee and Sreya Maitra Roychoudhury

Introduction

An autobiography of Indian foreign policy would showcase persistent navigation through the vicissitudes of international politics and complex structural and ideational factors for decades, as a prelude to being poised today as a major power seeking to claim its legitimate position in the world order. International relations' scholars have interpreted the foreign policy narrative in various styles, often identifying phases, roughly coinciding with the major historical events and premiership of successive leaders. A structure-agency reading locates the conditioning influence on India's foreign policy in the signals originating from the structure or systemic context. Foreign policy in turn elicits responses from the structure, notwithstanding the ideational, political and cultural factors which often qualify these structural signals.

While this paper does not wish to attempt yet another interpretation as such, it does seek to develop a discourse based on the disjuncture between post-Independence and post-Cold War foreign policies in India, identify the indices of ideology, norms and principles, and material capabilities which correspond to, and illustrate this shift, only to highlight the post-colonial elements that continue to shape, and in many ways limit India's foreign policy choices. The paper pins power and normativity as the dual registers of Indian foreign policy that interact in myriad ways. It asserts that despite its attempts to emerge as a major international power in the post-Cold War era, Indian foreign policy continues to remain mired in its post-colonial anxieties of gaining symmetry among territorial sovereignty, democracy and human rights.

The strong diplomatic moves under Prime Minister Narendra Modi's leadership apparently offer glimpses of a confident and invigorated stance, though its real and tangible impact on the theoretical trajectory of India's foreign policy is yet to carve itself out. The existence of a 'Modi doctrine' is under debate (Hall, 2015), indicating the success of his leadership; but the nature of concerns reveal remarkable continuity with the past.

The paper evolves through the following sections. Section I outlines India's post-Independence foreign policy; section II discusses the end of the Cold War and a new power imagination; section III outlines India's forays into new multilateralism; section IV highlights the post-colonial anxieties and their limitations; the final section offers concluding comments.

Section I: India's Post-Independence Foreign Policy

For an expert on the sinews of India's foreign policy today, the post-Independence *avatar* which held ground till the end of the Cold War seems almost pristine in its contours and thrust. This phase had its moorings in the contesting realities and aspirations which drove post-Independent India. Freedom from the British after decades of intense nationalist struggle had accorded India remarkable prestige at the world stage, hailing not only its successful crusade against colonialism, imperialism and racism, but also as a champion of decolonization, people's rights and justice against arbitrary power. The first generation of politicians to take the mantle of government under the leadership of Prime Minister Jawaharlal Nehru was quick to decide in favour of retaining and entrenching this image of India. As Ramchandra Guha points out, for Nehru, foreign policy was a means of making India's presence felt in the world. Through his long tenure, he simultaneously served as the foreign minister of the Government of India. He personally supervised the creation of the Indian Foreign Service, transferring to its cadre, able officers of the Indian Civil Service and making fresh selections from the young (Guha, 2012; 151-178). Sumit Ganguly infers that at a personal level, Nehru sought to pursue an *ideational* foreign policy (Ganguly, 2010:1), and thus, the overall rubric had found its mould.

The ideas which soon emerged as the foundational principles of Indian foreign policy were pioneering, drawing on Indian tradition and political thought. Stephen Cohen infers that the examination of historical records makes Indians draw two conclusions; first, that the accomplishments of the great Indian Hindu rulers of the past, and even some of the deeds of the Muslims and the British are 'second to none'. The richness of ancient Indian philosophical and political thought, the profundity of its religions, the mastery of mathematics, science, and the developments of a complex social and political order at a time when Europeans were organized into primitive tribe, are the distinguished features of a great world civilization.

Related to this, and secondly, the historical memory of a great Indian civilization has practical consequences; the Indian officials believe that they are representing not just a state but a unique civilization, which has something special to offer to the rest of the world. Cohen argues that these beliefs explain Nehru's tendency to moralize, and the Indian propensity to lecture other powers, great and small (Cohen, 2013: 65-66).

However, deliberating on the sources of the strategic ideas which guide Indian foreign policy, Pant and Bajpai point out that although canonical texts such as the Hindu Vedas, Upanishads, Puranas, *Manusmriti* or epics such as the Ramayana, Mahabharata and Bhagavad Gita, and Kautilya's *Arthshastra* are often cited as the influences on India's strategic thinking, for the elite Indian involved in the articulation and implementation of foreign policy 'to bring to bear a deep knowledge even of the Hindu epics would be surprising' (Pant and Bajpai, 2013: 4). They are more assured of the influences of first generation politicians like C.

Rajagopalachari, Ram Manohar Lohia, K.M. Panikkar (in addition to Nehru), and civil servants, academicians, military academies (National Defence College, Indian Military Academy) and other civilian institutions (Indian Council of World Affairs, Institute for Defence Studies and Analyses) (Pant and Bajpai, 2013: 5).

Similarly, J.N. Dixit notes that self-perception of India's historical identity was selective and normative, concretized through concepts of tolerance, non-aggression, a commitment to reason in resolving controversies, conflicts, an acknowledgement of the supreme virtue of nurturing peace through a non-expansionist and non-acquisitive approach. This was a selective, self-adulating, 'motivated' perception, based on what 'we as people collectively thought, was good for our survival and socio-economic well-being in a complex, competitive world' (Dixit, 2010: 22). The ideas which guided Indian foreign policy in the immediate post-Independence period were thus not unequivocally hinged on norms alone; they were conscious of a realist goal.

Writings of Jawaharlal Nehru repeatedly articulated India's demands to be recognized as a great power despite opposition from the established powers of the world (Brecher, 1968). Itty Abraham (Abraham, 1998) notes that the need to gain global recognition of India's importance was also rooted in Nehru's insistence that newly independent countries must have a say in world affairs. He believed (and soon most of the Indian establishment came to believe) that it lay within India's diplomatic prowess to mould the external environment to suit its national purpose. The effort to establish India as a forceful and independent voice in international fora became a driving concern (Koithara, 1999: 59).

Thus, a unique mix of normative principles asserting India's civilizational history, penchant for peace, neutrality, development, justice and national strength became the necessary basis for conducting external relations and foreign policy. In addition to the tenets of anti-imperialism, anti-colonialism and a rejection of racialism, Indian foreign policy consolidated around the tenets of non-alignment, peaceful co-existence, temper of peace and friendship, disarmament and dedicated support to the United Nations Organization (UN). A brief discussion of these foundational principles would be pertinent, before analyzing their efficacy in *realpolitik*.

The meaning of non-alignment as Nehru conceived it was, meant not tying yourself up with military blocs of nations or with a nation. It means trying to view things as far as possible, not from the military point of view, though that has to come in sometimes, but independently and trying to maintain friendly relations with all countries. The policy of non-alignment thus implied that India has no military alliances with countries of either bloc; an independent foreign policy, not being tied down to a particular line of action through the membership of a bloc; maintaining friendly relations with all countries.

Also non-alignment *did not* mean a few things; it did not exclude close relationships with countries in terms of friendly cooperation; it did not mean neutrality as this term suggests no positive opinion on issues dividing the blocs, while India has displayed the diametrically opposite attitude. Nehru specified that 'though we are unaligned and uncommitted to military blocs, but are committed to various policies, various urges, objectives, principles and very much so' (Nehru Lok Sabha Debates, November 22, 1960). Thus, the doctrine of non-alignment called for steering a diplomatic path free from superpower dominance. Also, the moral stance of non-alignment against colonization and apartheid neatly dovetailed with India's Gandhian heritage (Ganguly, 2010: 1).

The principles of non-alignment and peaceful coexistence found consolidation in the *Panchsheel*—five-fold principles of mutual respect for territorial integrity and sovereignty, non-aggression, non-interference in domestic affairs of another country, equality and mutual benefit and peaceful co-existence, formulated in the context of the Tibetan crisis between India and China in 1954. The emphasis on global peace also turned India into a strong advocate of complete disarmament, with nuclear disarmament being accorded the highest priority. The country played a vital role in the UN peacekeeping operations, supplying missions in the Middle East, Cyprus, Congo and Zaire. It highlighted the issue of decolonization in the United Nations (UN) General Assembly and introduced along with Ireland, the first standstill resolution at the UN in 1954 calling for complete cessation of nuclear testing (Ganguly, 2010: 2). India was also noted for its efforts to draw international attention to the problems of economic development in the General Assembly and playing an active role in UN deliberations on the creation of a more equitable international economic order. Other issues such as environmentally sustainable development and promotion and protection of human rights were also important issue areas of focus in India's foreign policy at the UN platform.

However, a closer observation of these principles and their context reveal that the normative overlay was not devoid of a realist, instrumentalist crux, and this was evident on dual counts. First, India's foreign policy needed to manoeuvre a respectable, independent path befitting its sovereign status, in an international matrix replete with superpower dominance and the growing chill of the Cold War. Secondly, domestic weaknesses in terms of its economy, nascent democratic setting, federal execution of power, regional pulls and pressures and feeble military capabilities necessitated a foreign policy of peace, non-violence and neutrality. A typical realist reading would explain that, as a self-help unit in the international system with limited capabilities vis-à-vis other, more powerful state-units, India's survival necessitated entrenching its sovereign territoriality while defining its core national interests. Thus, Indian foreign policy found its anchor in bold normative pronouncements, implicitly cognizant of the growing power and materialistic needs of a just-sovereign nation, as measured in the realist paradigm. Nehru himself seemed to have acknowledged the role of both ideas and interests by stating that morality and self-interest direct Indian foreign policy (Power, 1964: 270).

Asserting non-alignment as an explicitly realist policy choice, Srinath Raghavan contends that Nehru stressed from the beginning that non-alignment embodied pragmatism as much as the principle. He observed that it was "not a wise policy to put all our eggs in one basket...purely from the point of view of opportunism...an independent policy is the best" (Raghavan, 2010: 20). But Raghavan conceded that later, Nehru increasingly began to couch the idea of non-alignment in the language of morality and principles and attracted criticism for mismatch between his rhetoric and actions (Raghavan, 2010: 20). This provides us with a convenient handle to explore how the power matrix may have cast its spell on normativism in India's foreign policy.

There seem to be two distinct ways: broadly, these are the *realpolitik* compulsions of the external and internal environments and limitations in capabilities which Nehru and other leaders were acutely mindful of. The argument at this level is that the normative high-ground aided India's distance from any drain of already paltry resources for gaining a *locus standi* in international politics. And secondly, the drawbacks of these principles in managing contentious elements in foreign relations soon brought India face to face with regional wars, which discredited their efficacy. In other words, the apparent strength of a foreign policy based on moral principles was betrayed by turbulent world politics and bloc-alliances, together with inadequacies in overall military preparedness. Nehru was aware of the limitations India faced during its immediate post-Independence period (Nehru, 1960: 9).

Given its constraints as a nascent democracy and a developing country in the Cold War world, non-alignment and peaceful co-existence as foreign policy strategy made rational sense. Commensurate with its material weakness, India sought to espouse its soft-power resources, particularly by means of ideology and international morality, to establish a leadership position among developing countries. Justifying non-alignment, Nehru said on December 4, 1947: I have no doubt that fairly soon, in the course of two or three years, the world would find this attitude justified and India will not only be respected by the major protagonists in the struggle for power, but a large number of smaller nations which today are rather helpless will probably look to India more than to other countries for a lead in such matters...(*Ibid*, 11).

Nehru's understanding of the concept was very different from the standard realist discourse of the same. He believed, therefore whether a country is imperialist or socialist on communist, its foreign ministers thinks primarily of the interests of that country. But there is a difference, of course. Some people may think of the interests of their country, regardless of their consequences. Others may think that in the long-term, the interest of another country is as important to them as that of their own country...self-interest may itself demand a policy of cooperation with other nations, goodwill for other nations...(Rana, 1967: 95).

The policy of non-alignment served two further and essential purposes. First, it put India along with states wishing to be independent and sovereign in international affairs. Second, non-alignment was a security insurance against the adverse consequences of the balancing process.

Nehru argued that in international affairs, there were no permanent friends. Therefore, non-alignment was a way of hedging bets. Non-alignment was not only a policy of exercising restraint on existing hegemonic powers, but also a check on prospective hegemonic outfits. Seen from such a perspective, "there was hardly any contradiction in taking Western help when attached by a hegemonic power like China, whilst continuing to oppose any marked extension of Western influence in Asia, especially in the immediate vicinity of India ...(Nehru, 1968). These statements make it clear that some of the elements of pragmatism embedded in the current definition of co-existence and in the current exposition of Indian foreign policy strategy have their roots in Nehruvian thought (Gupta and Chatterjee, 2015: 105-106).

Scholars also point out that non-alignment had effectively shielded India's fragile economy from outside forces as it erected its modern infrastructure. But the failure to improve agricultural productivity forced India to seek concessional PL 480 food aid from the U.S. in 1958—the Aid Consortium of Western Donors under the US leadership was created. By the late 1950s, India had become the biggest aid recipient of not just the US but also from the US-dominated World Bank (Koithara, 1999: 61).

Hagerty and Hagerty claim that till 1962, New Delhi pursued what may be termed as *true non-alignment;* that is, it attempted to have friendly relations with all three of the most important external powers; China, the United States and Soviet Union. Also, in a pragmatic way, India formalized and consolidated earlier British-Indian ties with Bhutan, Nepal, Sikkim, Burma and Ceylon through post-Independence treaties. Thus, the Indo-Bhutan Treaty of Friendship (1949), Indo-Sikkim Treaty of Peace (1950), Indo-Nepal Treaty of Peace and Friendship and Treaty for Trade and Commerce (1950), Treaty of Friendship with Burma (1951) and the Indo-Ceylon Agreement on Iimmigration (1954) ensured India's strategic commitment with all South Asian neighbours, excepting Pakistan.

Another factor which aided the trajectory of policy at this phase was that the leadership had a free hand in the conduct of foreign policy. In part, this is due to the lack of effective parliamentary restraints on the prime minister; to the inability of associational groups to mobilize popular support on foreign policy questions; to the lack of a bipartisan tradition between the ruling party and the opposition; to the pervasive view that criticism of official policy is somehow illegitimate; and, finally, to the dominance of a single party at the centre. However, there are examples when foreign policy moves were at variance with the ideological consensus of political elites. Nehru's handling of relations with China in the late 1950s is a classic Indian example of the government moving out of step with political elites.

Voices of concern were expressed regarding Chinese intentions in the mid-1950s after its occupation of Tibet and the publication of official Chinese maps showing as Chinese, some fifty thousand square kilometres of territory considered Indian (Andersen, 1983: 48).

True non-alignment was 'shattered' by the 1962 Chinese attack which laid bare India's weaknesses and the perils of going it alone in world politics (Hagerty and Hagerty, 2005: 41). Linking the ideas of non-violence and peace with the avoidance of war in domestic politics, Nehru had neglected the build-up of military power and curtailed spending on defence forces, to focus more on internal economic development. As Cohen puts it, Nehru brought to office a strong distaste for armed forces and military. He scathingly called them the 'merchants of death' and believed that the Indian Army had been a tool of the Raj, and thus, was not to be trusted (Cohen, 2001: 128).

Moreover, the victories of the armed forces in the domestic sphere, as manifest in the absorption of the princely states of Hyderabad (1948) and to invade and absorb Portugal's Indian colonies, most notably Goa, kept the political leadership confident of their ability to tackle emergencies, while carefully couching the avoidance of external military confrontation in the idiom of non-alignment and peaceful co-existence. But the eventual confrontation with China in the 1962 War and the military stalemate with Pakistan over the already internationalized Kashmir issue in 1965, not only upset India's strategic security calculations, but lent an embarrassing jolt to the normative leanings in the foreign policy. Nehru's refusal to allow the policy of non-alignment to be prejudiced by arms deals and alliances was only compatible with India's own prime requirements upon the basis that its relations with the neighbours were good.

However, this was not the case (Calvocoressi, 2000, 513);

and the wars of 1962 and 1965 reiterated this realist, military concern. Moreover, as Verghese Koithara rues, these wars showed how little support India could muster against China and Pakistan, which were both outside the Non-Aligned Movement (Koithara, 1999: 62). The period from 1962 to 1991 witnessed *tilted non-alignment* as India's priorities on defence spending brought it closer to the US and Britain. As Washington drew back from South Asia with the onset of the 1965 Indo-Pakistan war, India allowed itself to become more dependent on the Soviet Union to meet its security needs. The leadership of Mrs. Indira Gandhi infused greater pragmatism and realist appraisal of national interests in both foreign and domestic policies, indicative through political intervention during the Bangladesh war of 1971, and the eventual signing of the Treaty of Peace, Friendship and Co-operation with the Soviet Union in that same year, the development of nuclear weapons and India's first nuclear test in 1974. During 1965-1990, over eighty five percent of the major weapon systems that the Indian armed forces acquired were either imported from the Soviet Union or license-produced in India with Soviet assistance (Koithara, 1999: 66).

The tactical move away from non-alignment was visible in the aftermath of the Sino-Indian war. Politically conceived non-alignment, unsupported by strategically structured economic and security designs, deteriorated into non-engagement (Koithara, 1999: 62). Atul Kohli also argues in a similar vein that Indian leaders chose to advance the state as an effective agent of political order rather than as a successful facilitator of economic development; they built long chains of patronage that extended from the centre to the periphery, but undermined more egalitarian ambitions like land redistribution and the capacity to tax the agrarian sector (Kohli, 2004: 261). The long-run growth rate of the Indian economy over the period 1951-52 and 1981-82 was 3.5 percent; low savings rate and meagre foreign exchange reserves accounted for the slow growth rate. Even when investment rates picked up, the incremental capital-output ratios also went up, reflecting the rising economic inefficiencies (Varshney, 2013: 294-295).

In its formal discourse, however, the Indian foreign policy establishment never abandoned the rhetoric of non-alignment and peaceful co-existence. Raja Mohan though asserts that the inertia of non-alignment continued in India's public pronouncements more as a matter of routine and without any sense of the old fire (Raja Mohan, 2013: 30). However, India continued to champion the principles of decolonization, economic empowerment of the developing countries, and greater political say of the Third World countries in international affairs. The decolonization that proceeded rapidly in the 1960s had created a numerical majority of the Third World in the UN General Assembly; this gave leadership of the developing world, particularly India, the sense of opportunity to set the agenda for the world community and challenge the impregnable dominance of the West over international political discourse.

The NAM Summit in Lasaka, Zambia in 1970 gave the clarion call for a new international economic order that demanded a radical reordering of the terms of trade between the West and the developing world, and an expansion of the economic sovereignty of the Third World. The Algiers Summit in 1973 called for a new international information order, demanding an end to Western dominance in international flows (Raja Mohan, 2013: 36).

Section II: End of Cold War and a New Power Imagination

The end of the Cold War and the winding down of the super-power rivalry dramatically altered the imperatives of Indian foreign policy. The calculations and contours of policy so familiar to the Indian foreign policy elite informed primarily by the support, or interest, of the Soviet Union were rendered disarrayed. A major structural threat was also levelled by pivots of the unipolar power—the United States, and its allies. The initial period of the post-Cold War saw a dramatic withdrawal of great power involvement from South Asia, as a consequence of unprecedented events in Europe. The American perspective on South Asia, after the tumultuous events of the Gulf crisis and the initial buzz of activities in the Middle East to find a just solution to the Arab-Israeli conflict, came to settle on rather narrow non-proliferation concerns, with democracy and human rights being other, less serious, concerns.

As Kanti Bajpai observes in retrospect, "These entities could punish India diplomatically (in the United Nations, for example, on an issue like Kashmir), militarily (by denying it kcy technology), and economically by withholding multilateral funding (from the World Bank or IMF) or impeding private investment flows" (Bajpai, 1998: 176). Thereafter, systemic and unit level variables consistently combined to shape Indian responses in the post-Cold War era.

As external trends unfolded, each of the pillars of the Nehruvian paradigm—secularism, pluralism, mixed economy and socialism—were thoroughly contested. The device of neo-liberal economic policies were in part a response to international systemic pressures, as the dominant powers did not approve of the continuation of the plan-model any longer, and the dependence of the national economy on international facilities—a natural corollary to globalization—closed the option of autarkic, self-sufficiency-oriented economic policies before the state. The spectacular economic growth of China, that enabled her to become the second most significant power within the global hierarchy by the end of the last millennium, further contributed to building a domestic elite consensus on introduction of market reforms to propel India into an economic powerhouse within a relatively short period of time.

Security scenario was jeopardized not only by the loss of Soviet support but also with the waning of India's relations with the Clinton administration and Washington's ties with Pakistan and China becoming better. Inder Kumar Gujral, the then Indian ambassador to Moscow, summarized the Indian response in the following way: 'Perestroika and the new Soviet foreign policy offered us the prospects of dealing with both East and West without affecting our close and purposeful relations with the USSR. The strategy and nuances of these dealings have to be worked out carefully with one point in mind: our policy must, under no circumstances, smack of opportunism or dilute our time-tested friendship with the USSR' (quoted in Chari *et al.*, 2003: 15).

To carve a new power imagination, constrained by the logic of structural unipolarity, India now resorted to a curious mixture of bandwagoning and balancing vis-à-vis the United States. [1] During the Iraq War of 1991, India supported the US-led coalition in broad terms. It allowed US planes to refuel from its air bases despite domestic dissent. Post-9/11, once again India supported the US action in Afghanistan. After 2001, India's difference with the P-5 States over its positions on CTBT and the NPT also became narrower. It began to signal its willingness to sign these instruments if the P-5 States were willing to accept it within their ranks, with similar prestige and responsibilities.

Most conspicuous of bandwagoning behaviour has been its vote against Iran on the nuclear issue. However, on other issues, it continued to differ with the US-led West. It did not support the US war against Iraq in 2003, although it did not openly demonstrate any hostility either. There still remain problems over the issue of obtaining a permanent seat in the United Nations Security Council, and over the ambit or scope of its nuclear programme. As Kanti Bajpai notes, India seems to prefer a strategy of internal balances to become militarily strong enough to resist entanglements (Bajpai, 1998: 178).

Though India understands that this new-forged partnership with the US is a means to preserve American dominance in the Asian balance of power, open greater opportunities for American companies eager to exploit the vast potential of a rapidly growing Indian economy, and lend evidence to the American version of a partnership of democratic states, its ultimate value is that it helps New Delhi to expand its national power. Although this growth in capabilities leads India inexorably to formally demand a 'multipolar world, the leadership in New Delhi is realistic enough to understand that American primacy is unlikely to be dethroned any time soon and certainly not as a result of the growth in Indian power' (Tellis, 2005: 8). It is felt that issues and areas where India would want to project this power are consistent with US interests or, definitely would not contradict them. [2]

However, that India manoeuvres its *locus standi* in the unipolar international affairs through its own agency, is brought to fore by several factors. The idea of non-alignment, under the guise of 'strategic autonomy', the poverty of imagination arising out of its paucity of trained international affairs specialists, uncertainties induced by the political compulsions of coalition politics, modalities of dealing with Iran's quest for nuclear weapons, and India's firm resistance to any 'unilateral exercise of U.S. military power against recalcitrant regimes' (Ganguly, 2012: 6).

The post-Cold War period has also lent a renewed garb to India's relationship with China. While their power competition is inevitable, this rivalry would have to be managed in a world of myriad interdependent ties and economic linkages, where the spoils would have to be carefully invested into the relationship to ensure that none of the players succeed in leveraging the benefits unilaterally. This is an exceedingly complex challenge for both the states and India's great power potential would hinge significantly on how she manages her relations with her sprawling and powerful northern neighbour. India's power imagination in foreign policy strategy needs to thus, be mindful of both structural constraints and an explicit great power ambition that invests the agency with significant autonomy often at variance with its actual capability or the degree of external opposition. As Bajpai puts it, 'Indian decision-makers do not appear relentlessly preoccupied with power and its deployment. Indeed, they repeatedly turn to other resources and methods' (Bajpai, 1998: 194).

No great power can emerge without negotiating its immediate neighbourhood. Though in the post-Cold War world, India adopted certain measures like the 'Look East Policy' in 1991 to generate stronger economic interdependence and offered more concessions to its smaller neighbours in South Asia, India's rise unfortunately is not met by legitimacy within the South Asian context. The accusation points to India's insensitivity and arrogance, born of power. As Mitra and Schottli point out, the lack of regional trade, the traditional ganging-up of the smaller countries against the perceived bully, India, and the involvement of 'external actors' such as China and the United States have long been obstacles to Indian hegemony in the subcontinent—real or perceived. In consequence, the brand recognition of Indian foreign policy oscillates between that of a regional bully and a regional push-over (Mitra and Schottli, 2007: 30-31).

Moreover, the question of legitimacy is two-fold here and this complicates matters in South Asia. Indian foreign policy is susceptible to federal concerns and as coalition politics becomes the entrenched norm of the polity, national policies are therefore difficult to sell from the capital. They require provincial endorsement on critical matters and the demand for domestic legitimacy often trumps over its external counterpart. At the turn of the new century, for example, with tensions with Pakistan getting heightened over Kashmir, Western observers showed scepticism about India's ability to take hard decisions which could be denounced as appeasement in the domestic front (Anderson, 2001: 773-774).

Prime Minister Narendra Modi's style of foreign engagement has been noteworthy in this respect. As Brahma Chellaney shrewdly points out, with the invitation extended to all South Asian regional leaders at his swearing-in ceremony in May 2014, Modi rendered clear his priority to regain India's 'lost ground in the backyard' (Chellaney, December 2014). An impromptu and 'friendly' visit to Prime Minister Nawaz Sharif in Pakistan in December 2015 was preceded by extensive, scheduled, high-profile trips to Bhutan, Nepal, Bangladesh, Mongolia, South Korea, Afghanistan, Singapore, Malaysia, the United Arab Emirates and various countries of Central Asia throughout the year.

However, at the same time, in an overt endorsement of diplomatic symbolism, he remained non-committal to Pakistan in November 2014 during the SAARC Summit, when the latter refused to prosecute the masterminds of the Mumbai terror attacks. Mr. Modi shook hands with Mr. Sharif only the following day at the Dhulikhel retreat. He has also tried to institutionalize the idea of Asian solidarity', defined through three key markers; the Regional Comprehensive Economic Partnership (RCEP), a cyber-security architecture for the ASEAN Regional Forum, and the settlement of disputes through multilateral rules.

On maritime concerns in Asia, Mr. Modi has calibrated the Indian position, without straying too far from the traditional line. The India-Japan Joint Statement of 2015 referred to as "Indo-Pacific", officially brought this strategic phrase into India's foreign policy lexicon. However, the Prime Minister's speeches on the subject themselves allude to the Asia Pacific and Indian Ocean as distinct regions connected by history and destinies, "however we choose to define them" (Sukumar, December 2015). Thus, as India struggles to settle on national narrative(s) of foreign policy moves, its search for external legitimacy in the neighbourhood continues to remain increasingly complex and challenging.

Section III: New Multilateralism

India had in the past, mostly staked its international standing on multilateral institutions, such as the non-aligned movement, the UNCTAD, and the UN General Assembly. The post-Cold War era saw its entry into the World Trade Organization (WTO). The primary aim in these institutions has remained as one of securing national economic and security interests. India has also entered into formal and informal coalitions with several developing countries such as Brazil, China, Indonesia, and South Africa to serve specific purposes such as gaining time to modernize targeted sectors while providing protection to key domestic constituencies. Cohen observes that a clear shift in negotiating strategies at the multilateral forums was a clear indication that India wanted to get rid of its traditional image as a country that 'can't say yes' (Cohen, 2001: 66-91).

India's foreign policy had historically based itself on the idea of strategic autonomy and autarkic economic policies—but the underlying theory of interdependence in the post-Cold War world does not allow the same degree of autonomy. Moreover, unipolarity, impinges critically on the workings of the multilateral institutions of which India is a part, and the logic of the system-transformation, in terms of polarity, has already turned some of them merely ornamental. While India no doubt benefits from multilateralism and interdependence, it also faces the challenge of gaining sufficient autonomy under unipolarity—the norms on interdependence and other issues are shaped primarily by the hegemon and its allies rather than by the other members of the international system. Thus, India's search for power through multilateralism remains delicate—it seeks to engage the support of the United States where their vital interests converge, and explores alternative modes to push her interests where they clash with American priorities.

The post-Cold War reality has forced India to articulate a sense of *positive autonomy*, and work out how to navigate the global order under the new circumstances. Despite these challenges, most Indian scholars (Mehta, 2009) are convinced that only interdependence and multilateral engagement can open up new opportunities for India. Thus, certain institutions that India avoided in the earlier era are now engaged with. Institutions like the IMF, World Bank and the General Agreement on Tariff and Trade (GATT), which earlier did not bring much tangible security or material benefits to India have now emerged as locations of contestation where the emerging economies such as Brazil, China and India have sought reforms to make these institutions more reflective of the economic realities of the current times.

Consistent with the demands of a more rule-based order which India has championed since its post-Independence days, Indian policy-makers continue to play a role in conflict management and to seek major structural and functional reforms of the UN and other international organizations. This approach towards multipolarity, in general, and the UN, in particular, continues despite a belief that "India gives much to the United Nations, but gains very little from it" (Sreenivasan, 2009: 475). One can argue then that India's consistent support of the UN is an area where India overlooks its short-term gains in favour of pursuing a long-term normative goal of establishing a rule-based global order. Despite a lack of reciprocal advantages, India has taken part in forty three out of a total of sixty eight peacekeeping operations the UN has undertaken since 1948 (Ministry of External Affairs, India; UN Peacekeeping Operations Fact Sheet, 2013). It remained as one of the top three troop and other personnel contributors in 2013 (United Nations Peacekeeping, 2013).

India has pursued its claim for a permanent membership in the Security Council on the basis of its civilizational legacy, its status as the world's largest and most vibrant democracy and the fourth largest economy in terms of purchasing power parity. Its claim further arises from its unswerving commitment to the ideals and activities of the UN and its impressive record of participation in UN peacekeeping operations. While these bases of claim arise from a "narrow major-power claim", India's earliest advocacy of UN reform comes from a normative position on the representativeness of UNSC and pre-dates India's rise as an emerging power (Malone and Mukherjee, 2013: 114). India anchors its claim to the permanent seat not only as part of the G-4 (Germany, Japan, Brazil and India) but also as an active member of L-69, a larger coalition of developing countries advocating the UN reforms.

Given the state of reforms currently, one can argue that India and its partners have been somehow successful in tweaking the rules according to which quotas and votes are assigned to IMF member countries. In pursuing these paths, India's foreign policy demonstrates that it accepts the existing international order while it works within the system to change some of the norms. It does not seek to pursue transformational goals, although the BRICS proposal to set up a bank for infrastructure funding could be perceived as one. India's goal in working with other BRICS countries is to strengthen support for reform of multilateral institutions. Prime Minister Singh has repeated this point on several occasions. Speaking at Sanya, China at the third BRICS Summit, Singh said, "we are embarked on a major enterprise of socio-economic change for our peoples. Cooperation among BRICS holds the promise of building an external environment for ourselves that helps each of us and complements our task of nation building". Speaking at the joint press conference, Singh reiterated "(a)n important objective must remain the reform of institutions of global governance to make them truly representative of contemporary realities". The same themes were repeated at Yekaterinburg, New Delhi and elsewhere.

The tug between vital national interest and investing in the legitimacy of global commons as a responsible rising power marks India's foreign policy choices over a wide range of issues such as nuclear non-proliferation, the WTO negotiations or the climate talks, where considerations of national interest have more often triumphed over the latter. In this vein, a new cause for concern promoted by Prime Minster Modi has been the emphasis on cyber policies. At intergovernmental venues like ASEAN, BRICS or the G20, Mr. Modi has highlighted the importance of securing cyber networks from state and non-state actors. At the East Asia Summit, markedly in the presence of China, the Prime Minister called for "norms of behaviour" in cyberspace. To the private sector, Mr. Modi has flagged "data privacy and security" as a key concern, notably during his visit to Silicon Valley in September.

Renewable energy is another area of priority for Modi, linking concerns of national interest and international engagement. Floating the idea of climate justice for the first time in the recently concluded Paris Climate Conference in December 2015, he argued that the "developed countries must fulfil their responsibility to make clean energy affordable and accessible to all in the developing world". He expressed the desire for the US$ 100 billion a year plan for assistance from the rich to poor nations by 2020 to be expedited. Mr. Modi demanded that the rich nations meet their obligations in a credible and transparent manner. Apparently referring to the pressure that countries like India may face under a Paris deal, he said he welcomed stock-taking that was done in a transparent manner, where it covered both support and commitment, based on the principle of differentiation. The UN's principles of equity and *common but differentiated responsibilities* should firmly underpin any formulation. Acknowledging the reality that conventional energy sources such as coal would continue to be used at present, the Prime Minister said funds were necessary to clean up coal-based generation. This could be done using the Green Climate Fund which needs scaling up (Ananthakrishnan, December 2015).

The Paris accord, in contrast to the climate negotiations in the past, has been more successful to set a consensual framework for effective carbon emission reduction after 2020. India played a major part towards the success of the Paris negotiations, though the results are hotly debated by experts on all sides. For one, India succeeded to hold on its traditional norm of common but differentiated responsibility that puts the major responsibility on developed nations to radically cut their carbon emissions and compensate the developing nations with infrastructure, finance and technology to help them transform into low carbon economies. Mr. Javadekar emphasized that the pact has unequivocally adopted the climate Justice. "We are happy that the agreement differentiates between the responsibilities of the developing and developed nations", he said (NDTV, December 13, 2015). The developed states are expected to raise US$ 100 billion annually by 2020, and push it up considerably in the following years.

Despite the deal, the issue of distribution of financial responsibility remains contentious and continues to divide the developed, fast developing and environmentally vulnerable states. The deal puts more onuses on the developed countries by asking them to hit zero emissions by 2020 but also *recognizes the need for greater support to developing countries to adopt more ambitious renewable energy plans.* In the words of Niharika Mandhana, "but some analysts say the agreement could indirectly restrict the ability of developing countries to use fossil fuels like coal that remain crucial to bringing power to millions of poor households for the first time and to industrializing further. That means India and other developing nations might find it more difficult to muster international financing for coal-fired power plants. For India and other fast-growing countries, banking on coal-powered development, this could pose a problem" (Mandhana, Niharika, 2015).

India claimed that the deal was neither a victory of the developed world nor that of the less developed; it was rather a victory for global climate. What is pertinent is the fact that while India has not radically budged from its traditional commitment to the norm of 'differentiated responsibility', it has shown greater pragmatism and played a crucial role in bridging the differences among various stakeholders that went a long way to clinch the Paris deal.

India's stand at the World Trade Organization (WTO) on the food-stockpiling issue—central to India's food security—is also significant. After vetoing the WTO's Trade Facilitation Agreement in Geneva, India made the US, climb down on the food-stockpiling issue and yet earned praise from Mr. Obama for helping to break the impasse. Even the head of the UN's International Fund for Agricultural Development, backed the veto, saying the real choice for India in Geneva was between "feeding" its citizens and "creating jobs" for wealthy economies. After all, the main providers of agricultural subsidies are the rich countries plus China (Chellaney, December 2014).

India reinforced its commitments to the developing world by pitching for a global trading regime that serves development goals and improves trade prospects together with African states. In Modi's words, "When we meet at Nairobi Ministerial of the WTO in December, we must ensure that the Doha Development Agenda of 2001 is not closed without achieving these fundamental objectives". Further, "we should also achieve a permanent solution on public stockholding for food security and special safeguard mechanism in agriculture for the developing countries" (Press Trust of India, October 2015).

The WTO's General Council, the highest decision-making body of the organization, gave in to India's demand for extending the peace clause until a permanent solution was clinched on the vexed food stockpiling issue. Another major gain for India was the decision by the WTO to decouple the negotiations to find a permanent solution on public stockholding from the other deliberations on agriculture and related subjects within a general framework.

In case of multilateralism in trade and economic matters, India has abandoned its previous strategy of always speaking out for developing countries, though it continues to strategically adopt such positions. During the Doha Round, India has built sectoral coalitions with states that have similar interests as opposed to focusing only on large, ideologically-based coalitions of the past—the trade G-20 coalition in agriculture is the best example of such a coalition. India continues to speak for developing country interests at the Fund-Bank meetings because India's high rates of poverty make some of its interests similar to the interests of poor countries. However, at those same Fund-Bank meetings, India also shares platform with Brazil and others in demanding higher quotas.

India's membership in developing country coalitions such as G-33 in the WTO or G-77 at the UN can also be seen as strategic moves—these allow India an opportunity to band together with China and other developing countries to put pressure on developed countries in the context of trade and climate negotiations. This is not a break from India's traditional position on the World Trade Organization's centrality to international trade. Themes of trade and energy trade partnerships have been a major theme in Mr. Modi's foreign policy interventions also. At the G-20 Summit in Antalya, he asserted this clearly, warning that regional agreements "should not lead to a fragmentation of the global trading system" (Sukumar, December 2015). This is also where one can observe ideational continuity in India's overall foreign policy strategy: the preferred role as a leader of like-minded and similarly situated states rather than an ally of the dominant powers of the global order.

India's role projection in international affairs has been consciously steered through new tools of explaining foreign policy. To that end, in 2006, India had created the Public Diplomacy Division within the Ministry of External Affairs, dedicated to manage and promote a positive image of India to the outside world. The novelty of new institution carried three-fold implications: it is actively seeking new audience within India, in the West and in the developing world; it is being more interactive and democratic by engaging the wider public of foreign relations issues and it is seeking to utilize new media rather than traditional methods (Hall, 2012: 1090; Kugiel, 2012: 360). According to the latest data available, as of 2013, the Public Diplomacy Division had 100,000 friends on Facebook, around 70,000 people on Twitter and about one million viewers on YouTube (Kugiel, 2012: 360).

Section IV: Post-colonial Anxieties

From the nadir of economic bankruptcy, domestic political

chaos and isolation in international politics with the loss of Soviet ally, India's push forward towards strategic posturing to brush shoulders with the great powers and vindicate its defined role in the post-Cold War world has no doubt marked a foreign policy makeover. And yet, there is more than what meets the eye. India's colonial baggage of experiences and post-colonial tasks of nation-building have tacitly imparted certain values and attitudinal references which continue to implicitly guide foreign policy overtures on many counts. These temper its involvement in many ongoing international initiatives, projects and major power investments. While there is no need for any sweeping value judgment on such a qualified stance in world affairs though seeking to carve its place as a major power, the identification of these post-colonial anxiety factors are significant nevertheless, as the substance of that hyphen between the matrices of power and norms which India is constantly seeking to converge in general, but complement at best.

Freedom House Report, 2013 gave India a freedom rating of 2.5, which is good (Freedom House, 2013). While India's commitment to democracy has indeed been very deep set, its involvement in promotion of democracies has been marginal at best. Despite being one of the oldest democracies of the world, and an example of a successful post-colonial democracy, India's wariness in democracy promotion has attracted attention and raised questions. Among some of the scholarly explanations for this contradiction, there is a consensus that India's position on international intervention remains consistent with Westphalian notions of sovereignty and non-intervention. Former Prime Minister Dr. Manmohan Singh stated in a speech at the United Nations General Assembly in September 2011 (in the aftermath of the Western intervention in Libya) that, "democratic, plural secular India can contribute to tolerance and peaceful co-existence among nations... [However], the observance of the rule of law is as important in international affairs as it is within countries. Societies cannot be reordered from outside through military force. People in all countries have the right to choose their own destiny and decide their own future" (India Today, 2011).

Scholars believe that this attitude is born out of India's deep-rooted aversion to colonialism and imperialism rooted in history, consciousness of the imperfectness of India's own democracy and its immediate neighbourhood that consists of a number of authoritarian regimes (Ganguly, 2013). Being fully cognizant of the fact that there is little capability to promote democracies in the region, Indian policy makers have remained similarly reticent in supporting democracy promotion efforts of the West in other parts of the world (Gupta and Chatterjee, 2015: 119).

Explaining the lack of democracy-promotion as a conscious foreign policy choice, Atul Mishra argues that unlike the US, India's democracy evolved in a non-industrial, complex socio-cultural, agrarian context, checkered with scarcity of opportunities and resources, and an affective relationship with the security of the land. Thus, Mishra contends that India's foreign policy cannot afford to promote democracy abroad by adopting an 'other-regarding' orientation; its democratic leanings in foreign policy remain, non-universal, self-regarding and to that extent, non-liberal (Mishra, 2012: 55).

S.D. Muni notices India's reticence in democracy-promotion since the beginning of the post-Independence period. He makes the following argument. India could have become the hub of democratic struggles and movements in Asia, especially South Asia, as the then Soviet Union and Communist China sought to do with regard to the communist movements. However, the creeping in of the Cold War, and China's emergence as a communist power radically transformed Asia's geo-strategic contours, making issues of security and stability more urgent and immediate than of internal political transformations. The alliance structures create serious obstacles in the way of nascent democratic initiatives in many countries.

Thus, the Indian political leadership and bureaucratic

establishment saw greater sense in pursuing security interests, rather than inserting in ideological expansion. While there was the natural preference for democracy, its promotion in Asia and the neighbourhood was not seen as an instrument of 'real' power. Also, India did not seem equipped to invest economic and diplomatic resources and bear the political costs and other risks involved (Muni, 2009: 128-130). But Muni points out that wherever India found the democracy factor conducive to its perceived strategic and security interests, it went all out to support, as witnessed in the creation of Bangladesh (1971), Nepal (1989) and Afghanistan (post-9/11) (Muni, 2009: 132). The agenda as such has benefited India's partnership with the US in the new millennium. Mallavarapu observes that as of now, India is keen on endorsing democracy-promotion if it is represented in India's own national interest, pursued selectively where the circumstances are appropriate, and in ways that command support at home.

Since the recent memories of the unacceptable and not just misguided attempt to impose 'regime change' on Iraq still weigh heavily, India is likely to continue to tread cautiously with regard to international democracy promotion. While it has conceded some ground already to minimalist multilateral initiatives, most notably in the form of being one of the founding members of the Community of Democracies in 2000, support for the UN Democracy Fund since 2010, and formal membership of it in 2005, underlying anxieties about the democracy-promotion project persist. While India is deeply committed to democracy at home, its belief in the principle of non-intervention in international affairs remains part of the common sense of its foreign policy. Moreover, Muni makes the valid point that India's efforts in these multilateral initiatives towards democracy promotion must be viewed in the context of the US-India *rapprochement* rather than as a genuine policy of exporting the Indian model of democracy (Muni, 2009). Democracy promotion in its most ugly avatar of regime change is unacceptable both to the political elite and the larger public in India. Thus, for the times being, it seems that India will continue to keep a low profile and hedge its bets carefully (Mallavarapu, 2010: 59-60).

Regarding interventions, the Indian government has opposed in recent years to intervention plans in Libya and Syria as well as its somewhat ambiguous position on the concept of responsibility to protect. On the one hand, India has resisted granting the UN Security Council, the authority to carry out actions consistent with the idea of humanitarian intervention. On the other hand, there is a groundswell of support among Indian diplomats for the position that the international community has a responsibility to prevent mass atrocities. As to possible responses to such atrocities, Indian policy makers have emphasized the primacy of peaceful attempts at crisis resolution and the use of sanctions (Ganguly, 2013). On these issues, the Indian position has tended to move closer to Russia's and China's and the Indian government has faced criticism and condemnation from the western powers and particularly, the western press (Mukherjee and Malone, 2013: 112; Chatterjee and Gupta, 2015).

A similar reluctance remains in promoting the cause of human rights. Here, the concern is that such promotion might redirect the spotlight on its own rather checkered history with upholding the rights of several minorities at home and its use of military, paramilitary and policy forces in dealing with insurgencies across the country (Gupta and Chatterjee, 2015: 119). The ongoing struggle of the ethnic communities in the North-East, the long-standing demand of the Kashmiris for autonomy and the Maoist challenge have been securitized by the state for consecutive decades now, causing unprecedented human rights violations and casualties. Millions of civilian casualties have been witnessed in these internal war zones across India. The *South Asian Terrorism Portal* registers 24,531 civilian casualties from 1994 to 2015 and 64,177 fatalities in total (SATPb, 2015). While Indian Tamils have been deeply affected by the civil war in Sri Lanka against the LTTE which concluded

only in 2009 after three decades, India abstained from voting in favour of an international investigation on Sri Lanka against the alleged war crimes and human rights' violations at the United Nations Human Rights Commission in 2014.

Mishra points out that liberal writings lament India's lack of strong positions against human rights violations including pogroms, semi-organized killings and genocides in undemocratic or illiberal societies. Its seeming indifference to evidently cruel and inhuman actions, witnessed in recent years in Myanmar, Sudan, Sri Lanka and Syria, is often underlined. This position is defended by some and criticized by others for its pragmatism or 'realism'. Assuming a somewhat self-critical prism, Mishra ascribes this tendency to be rooted in Indian cultural codes characterized by Brahminical social and cultural attitudes. Despite the avowal of a highly moral and lofty world view that may appear sympathetic to human life in general, Brahminism has perpetuated, and shown remarkable indifference to, cruelties against certain communities (Mishra, 2012: 55).

However, it must be added that as an aid donor, India has actively provided development assistance to countries in its immediate neighbourhood like Bangladesh, Nepal, Bhutan and the African countries, investing up to US$ 1.16 billion in 2013-2014 (Mullen, IDCR Report, 2014: 2). In 2014, Prime Minister Modi announced a US$ 1 billion line of credit for Nepal's infrastructure development in 2014. Mr. Modi also promised to help Nepal in the field of hydropower, infrastructure, space technology and agriculture (Jayshi and Haidar, August 2014).

In 2015, in a visit by an Indian Prime Minister for the first time, Modi announced a credit line of US$ 1 billion to Mongolia to expand its economic capacity and infrastructure, as they decided to upgrade their relationship from comprehensive to "strategic partnership". India and South Korea signed seven agreements, including on avoidance of double taxation and formalising consultations between National Security Councils of the two nations, to boost bilateral ties. India also raised the outlay provision for the Afghan Parliament to ₹ 969 crore from ₹ 710 crore (approved in June 2014) with the assurance of timely completion before December 31 (The Indian Express, December 2015). Whether these grants would yield any positive result for India remains to be seen. However, India has definitely become more proactive under the present dispensation in using grants, aid and facilitating pro-business deals both in its immediate neighbourhood and beyond to extend its influence further.

India, thus, has never been an unequivocal supporter of all global institutions. Malone and Mukherjee echo Pratap Bhanu Mehta's observation that India practices a foreign policy of "unprincipled moderation". While most countries practice double standards in expressing their values, India is notable for expressing few principles beyond that of "non-interference" in the affairs of others. However, its moderation of recent years is a major asset for international relations, not to be underestimated at the global level" (Malone and Mukherjee, 2011).

Conclusion

The paper has conducted a reading of India's foreign policy since the post-Independence period to analyze the manifestation, shifts, and turns of the distinct though not exclusive idioms of norms and power. The ideational rubric of foreign policy in the immediate post-Independence period, shaped through non-alignment, decolonization, anti-colonialism and anti-racialism have been outlined in the first section, while emphasizing their realist undertones for a struggling, post-colonial state in a world besieged by the Cold War. The post-Cold War realities and India's pro-liberal power imagination through selective engagement with great powers have been delineated in the next section, juxtaposing India's domestic political and economic compulsions with its ambitions to position itself as a major player.

India's multilateral initiatives have been focused upon in the third section which special emphasis on its role in the UN and WTO, highlighting the influence of the US and China on its decisions. The problems that India negotiates in its immediate neighbourhood have also been dwelt upon. The fourth section showcases India's predilection to hold on to its post-Independence norms of sovereignty and territoriality, its reticence in engaging with the West to promote any model of democracy. The discourse on India's stance on democracy-promotion despite trying to carve its niche in a unipolar world is delineated.

The paper concludes that there are two registers of Indian foreign policy, namely an aspiration to graduate into a major power and an ambivalent commitment to norms of multilateralism and a just world order. As a post-colonial state, India has always displayed a strong urge to bond with the Third World and maintained a complex relationship with the West. While the end of the Cold War introduced several new trends its dealings with the world, the tension between power and norms has survived. So far as the dominant and power-centric readings go, several points have emerged.

First, India has entered into a new phase in its foreign policy since the end of the Cold War and the US led military campaigns against terrorism. It has shed its ideological baggage of the Cold War, and become more pragmatic and self-confident in its dealings with the outer world. While it has not dumped non-alignment altogether, the geopolitical basis of that policy is gone. Its foreign policy is better couched as strategic autonomy that is more about multi-alignment rather than non-alignment. More critically, India is now a more active player of, and in the great power games and this is a qualitative shift in its foreign policy thinking and behaviour.

Second, economics drives some of the goals of India's foreign policy as never before. India believes that power flows from economic strength. The switch from a closed and state-controlled economic model to a liberalized and open trading order has vastly increased the significance of the international economic order for India's foreign policy. It is no longer an obstructive economic player; but a constructive economic power that seeks to realize its economic goals before anything else.

Third, India sees itself as a rising major power, if not a great power, and has significant hard and soft power resources, though a lot more needs to be done to improve its international standing. Fourth, there is the view that India remains a defensive actor and lacks sufficient status or reputation within the international order. Hence, India is neither a consistently status-quo power nor a thoroughly revisionist one. Finally, it is evident that India is mired in a difficult geo-strategic environment in its immediate neighbourhood and its success in dealing with some of these challenges has been rather limited.

However, if India's foreign policy has taken a decidedly realist turn, its normative commitments to multilateralism, democracy and a just or equitable world order constitute the second register of its international role. The point is that India remains a state mired in post-colonial anxieties, with strong commitments to sovereignty, territoriality, non-intervention, on one hand, and a democratic, non-hegemonic international order on the other. The complex interplay of these two registers condition India's foreign policy, moderating its realism and obfuscating its normative commitments at the same time. Hence, India's new international coalitions are diverse; it bonds with major developing states like Brazil and South Africa and partners with Japan, the US and the European Union at the same time. Its complex rivalry and cooperation with China reinforces the same point. Even on normative issues, India's positions are ambivalent.

As a consistent post-colonial democracy, it refrains from pursuing a strong democratic agenda in world politics. Though a functioning democracy, India's record of protecting the rights of its citizens remains deeply contested. Hence, despite occasional lip services to norms like responsibility to protect, India is deeply sceptical of bonding with the West on human rights. While its philosophy of economic development has decidedly taken a pro-liberal stand, it both supports and opposes the West in platforms like the WTO, depending on what its national interest demands. A similar duality manifests on issues of climate and environment where it prefers complex and shifting coalitions over fixed commitments. This may appear to be a decisive shift to realism. However, there is no linearity in India's external policies.

As this paper has sought to argue, India's normative commitments are not marginal to its power imagination; both power and norms of multilateralism remain central to its foreign policy. Prime Minister Modi's style of foreign policy has splashed new dynamics; he has sought to galvanize India's stance and image through the sheer volume of engagement, media pronouncements and proactive interventions. However, to what extent Modi's foreign policy is a break remains contested. Moreover, it cannot be denied, that the real fruits of his labour are yet to be witnessed. Taking a cue from the present trends, the embeddedness in norms is likely to continue unscathed; it will serve as the preferred premise for myriad, realist objectives of engagement and participation in international affairs.

Endnotes

1. Balance is to oppose or resist a dominant state or a coalition of states by domestic mobilization of resources, through countervailing external alliances, or by both. Bandwagoning, in contrast, is to join with the dominant power for security at a much lower cost.
2. The structural inspiration of this transformation is well captured by many scholars. Tellis writes, 'In this context, augmenting Indian power is judged to be essential to U.S. interests because it permits Washington to "pursue a balance-of power strategy among those major rising powers and key regional states in Asia which are not part of the existing U.S. alliance structure—including China, India, and a currently weakened Russia," a strategy that "seeks to prevent any one of these [countries] from effectively threatening the security of another [or that of the United States] while simultaneously preventing any combination of these [entities] from 'bandwagoning' to undercut critical U.S. strategic interests in Asia". (Khalilzad et al. 2001:47 cited in Tellis, 2005: 54-55).

References

Ananthakrishnan, G. (December 1, 2015), "Modi Asks Rich Nations to Cut Emissions, Share Carbon Space with Poor", *The Hindu*, accessed at: http://www.thehindu.com/sci-tech/energy-and-environment/cop21-paris-climate-conference-narendra-modi-cautions-against-unilateral-steps-in-combating-climate-change/article7933873.ece on 9th February 2016.

Andersen, Walter K. (Fall, 1983), "The Domestic Roots of Indian Foreign Policy", *Asian Affairs*, Vol. 10, No. 3, pp. 45-53, accessed at: http://www.jstor.org/stable/30172981 on 11th April 2015.

Andersen, Walter K. (September/October 2001), "Recent Trends in Indian Foreign Policy", *Asian Survey*, Vol. 41, No. 5, pp. 765-776, accessed at: http://www.jstor.org/stable/10.1525/as.2001.41.5.765 on April 11, 12015.

Abraham, Itty (1998), "The Making of the Indian Atomic Bomb: Science, Secrecy and the Post-colonial State", Post-colonial Encounters Series, London: Zed Books/New Delhi: Orient Longman.

Bajpai, Kanti (1998), "India: Modified Structuralism", in Muttiah Alagappa (ed.), 'Asian Security Practice: Material and Ideational Influences', Stanford and California: Stanford University Press, pp. 157-197.

Bajpai, Kanti and Harsh V. Pant (eds.) (2013), "India's Foreign Policy: A Reader", New Delhi: Oxford University Press.

Brecher, Michael (1968), "India and World Politics: Krishna Menon's View of the World", New Delhi: Oxford University Press.

Calvocoressi, Peter (2001), "World Politics: 1945-2000", New Delhi: Pearson Education.

Chari, P.R., Pervaiz Iqbal Cheema and Stephen Philip Cohen (2003), "Perception, Politics and Security in South Asia", London and New York: Routledge-Curzon.

Chellaney, Brahma (December 4, 2014), "Deconstructing the Modi Foreign Policy", *The Hindu*, accessed at: http://www.thehindu.com/opinion/lead/deconstructing-the-modi-foreign-policy/article6658904.ece on 9th February 2016.

Cohen, Stephen P. (2001), "India: Emerging Power", New Delhi:

Oxford University Press.

Freedom House (2013), "Freedom in the World 2013: Democratic Breakthroughs in the Balance", accessed at: https://freedomhouse.org/report/freedom-world/2013/india#.VTplytKqqko on 11th April 2015.

Ganguly, Sumit (2010), "The Genesis of Nonalignment", in Sumit Ganguly (ed.), 'India's Foreign Policy: Retrospect and Prospect', New Delhi: Oxford University Press, pp. 1-10.

Ganguly, Sumit (2012), "Think Again: India's Rise", *Foreign Policy*, July 5, Washington D.C., accessed at: http://www.foreignpolicy.com/articles/2012/07/05/think_again_india_s_rise?page=0,6 on 16 July 2012.

Ganguly, Sumit (2013), "India in the Liberal Order", paper presented at a workshop on India and the Liberal World Order, Transatlantic Academy, German Marshall Fund of the United States, Washington D.C.

Guha, Ramchandra (2012), "India after Gandhi: The History of the World's Largest Democracy", London: Picador.

Gupta, Surupa and Shibashis Chaterjee (2015), "Indian Foreign Policy and Coexistence: Continuity and Change in the post-Cold War Era", in Cedric de Coning, Thomas Mandrup and Lislotte Odgaard (eds.), 'The BRICS and Coexistence: An Alternative Vision of World Order', New York: Routledge.

Hagerty, Devin T. and Herbert G. Hagerty (2005), "India's Foreign Relations", in Devin T. Hagerty (ed.), 'South Asia in World Politics', USA: Rowman & Littlefield Publishers Inc., pp. 11-48.

Hall, Ian (2012), "India's New Public Diplomacy: Soft Power and the Limits of Government Action", *Asian Survey*, Vol. 52, No. 6, pp. 1089-1110.

Hall, Ian (2015), "Is a Modi Doctrine Emerging in India's Foreign Policy?", *Australian Journal of International Affairs*, 69:3, pp. 247-252.

India Today, "Full Text of Prime Minister Manmohan Singh's Speech at the UNGA", September 24, 2011, accessed at: http://indiatoday.intoday.in/story/manmohan-singh-speech-at-unga/1/152560.html on 24th April 2015.

Jayshi, Damakant and Suhasini Haidar (August 2014), "Modi Offers $ 1-bn package to Nepal", *The Hindu*, accessed at: http://www.thehindu.com/news/international/south-asia/narendra-modi-announces-nrs-10000-crore-as-concessional-line-of-credit-to-nepal-during-his-speech-at-constituent-assembly/article6277320.ece on 10th February 2016.

Kohli, Atul (2003), "State Directed Development: Political Power and Industrialization in the Global Periphery", United Kingdom: Cambridge University Press.

Koithara, Verghese (1999), "Society, State and Security: The Indian Experience", New Delhi: Sage.

Kugiel, Patryk (July and October 2012), "India's Soft Power in South Asia", *International Studies,* Vol. 49, Nos. 3 and 4, pp. 351-376.

Malone, David and Rohan Mukherjee (2011), "Polity, Security and Foreign Policy in Contemporary India", accased at: http://www.cerium.ca/IMG/pdf/Polity_Security_And_Foreign_Policy_In_Contemporary_India.pdf.

Mallavarapu, Sidhdharth (March 2010), "Democracy Promotion Circa 2010: An Indian Perspective", *Contemporary Politics,* 16: 1, 49-61, accessed at: http://dx.doi.org/10.1080/13569771003602895, April 19, 2015.

Mandhana, Niharika (2015), "How Will the Paris Climate Deal Impact Modi's Plan to Electrify India?", *The Wall Street Journal*, accaessed at: http://blogs.wsj.com/indiarealtime/2015/12/14/how-will-the-paris-climate-deal-impact-modis-plan-to-electrify-india.

Mehta, Pratap Bhanu (2009), "Still Under Nehru's Shadow? The Absence of Foreign Policy Frameworks in India", *India Review*, Vol. 8, No. 3, pp. 209-233.

Ministry of External Affairs (April 2015), "India and the United Nations," accessed at: http://www.mea.gov.in/india-and-the-united-nations.htm.

Mishra, Atul (2012), "India's Non-liberal Democracy and the Discourse of Democracy Promotion", *South Asian Survey*, 19(1), pp. 33-59, accessed at: http://sas.sagepub.com/content/19/1/33.

Mitra, Subrata K. and Jivanta Schottli (2007), "The New Dynamics of Indian Foreign Policy and its Ambiguities", *Irish Studies in International Affairs*, Vol. 18, pp. 19-34, accessed at: http://www.jstor.org/stable/25469813.

Mukherjee, Rohan and David M. Malone (July 2013), "India and the UN Security Council: An Ambiguous Tale", *Economic and Political Weekly*, XLVIII, No. 29, pp. 110-117.

Mullen, Rani D. (2014), "IDCR Report: The State of Indian Development Cooperation", Centre for Policy Research, accessed at: http://cprindia.org/Spring_2014_IDCR_Report_the_State_of_Indian_Development_Cooperation.pdf.

Nehru, Jawaharlal (November 1960), "Lok Sabha Debates in India's Foreign Policy: Selected Speeches", New Delhi: The Publications Division, Ministry of Information and Broadcasting, Government of India.

Nehru, Jawaharlal (1961), "India's Foreign Policy: Selected Speeches", New Delhi: The Publications Division, Ministry of Information and Broadcasting, Government of India.

NDTV (December 2015), "Historic Climate Deal: A Step to Better Future, Prakash Javadekar", accessed at: http://m.ndtv.com/india-news/historic-climate-deal-a-step-to-better-future-prakash-javadekar-1254261.

Power, Paul F. (April 1964), "Indian Foreign Policy: The Age of Nehru", *The Review of Politics,* Vol. 26, No. 2, pp. 257-286, accessed at: http://www.jstor.org/stable/1405752.

Press Trust of India (October 2015), "India to Seek Permanent Solution to Food Security Issue at WTO", accessed at: http://m.ndtv.com/india-news/india-to-seek-permanent-solution-to-food-security-issue -at-wto-1237717.

Raghavan, Srinath (2010), "War and Peace in Modern India", New Delhi: Permanent Black.

Raja Mohan, C. (2013), "Beyond Non-Alignment", in Kanti Bajpai and Harsh V. Pant (eds.), 'India's Foreign Policy: A Reader', New Delhi: Oxford University Press, pp. 27-50.

Rana, A.P. (1967), "Indian Non-alignment and the Balance of Power", in Paul F. Power (ed.), 'India's Non-alignment Policy: Strengths and Weaknesses', Boston: D.C. Heath and Company.

South Asian Terrorism Portal (2014), "Indian Fatalities", accessed at: http://cprindia.org/Spring_2014_IDCR_Report_the_State_of_Indian_Development_Cooperation.pdf.

Sreenivasan, T. (October/December 2009), "India at the United Nations: More Give than Take", *India Quarterly: A Journal of International Affairs*, 65: pp. 475-481.

Sukumar, Arun Mohan (December 2015), "A Shift from Style to Substance", *The Hindu*, accessed at:

http://www.thehindu.com/opinion/op-ed/modis-foreign-policy-a-shift-from-style-to-substance/article7987958.ece.

United Nations Peacekeeping (October 2013), "UN Peacekeeping Operations Fact Sheet," accessed at: http://www.un.org/en/peacekeeping/documents/bnote1013.pdf.

United Nations Peacekeeping (2014), "Troop and Police Contributors", accessed at: http://www.un.org/en/peacekeeping/resources/statistics/contributors.shtml.

Tellis, Ashley J. (2005), "India as a New Global Power: An Action Agenda for the United States", Washington D.C.: Carnegie Endowment for International Peace, pp. 11-59.

The Indian Express (December 2015), "Mapping PM Modi's Foreign Trips in 2015: 26 Countries So Far", accessed at: http://indianexpress.com/article/india/india-news-india/mapping-pm-modis-foreign-trips-in-2015-15-countries-and-now-russia.

Varshney, Ashutosh (2013), "Battles Half Won: India's Improbable Democracy", New Delhi: Penguin, Viking.

2

Emerging Vistas of India's Indo-Pacific Engagement

W. Lawrence S. Prabhakar

India's responses and options have been through the diplomatic processes of engaging with ASEAN with ARF and ADMM Plus, while simultaneously energize its Indian Ocean initiatives of Indian Ocean Rim Association and Indian Ocean Naval Symposium that could intensify engagement of Singapore, ASEAN states and East Asian powers like Japan, South Korea and Australia. This would also come with India's engagement with the Western Pacific Naval Symposium along with its economic and security diplomacy with Australia, New Zealand and the Pacific Islands Forum.

India is now emerging as a 'security provider' in the Asia-Pacific/Indo-Pacific region even as India expands its naval order of battle. India's expanding orders of battle in its armed forces specially its navy and air force with the emphasis on amphibious and expeditionary capabilities is increasing its capabilities, potential and performance to undertake a variety of operational missions that range from the coercive, compellance, benign and humanitarian operations within the region and beyond.

The "Aden to Malacca's" geographical swath of area now comes within the capabilities and reach of the Indian Navy. India's initiatives of the *Milan* and the Indian Ocean Naval Symposium *IONS* have accrued the institutional value addition to the prevalent ties and have fostered better naval engagement, providing India 'a naval corridor in the South China Sea all the way to the East Pacific' to engagements with

Japan, South Korea, Russia and the United States. India's naval engagement in the region would continue as a significant factor even as the PLA-Navy expansion and its surge into the Indian Ocean region continues. India's strategic engagement with the Southeast Asian and East Asian navies would be a counter-bulwark to the planned expansion in the region. Even as India expands its naval engagements with the United States, Japan, South Korea, Russia and Australia in the Eastern Pacific as well as in the Indian Ocean region, its role as a significant actor in the region enhances its credibility.

The paper endeavours to analyse: (a) the frameworks of understanding the Indo-Pacific region; (b) the systemic bases of India's Eastward economic and strategic engagement; (c) India's Asia-Pacific and Indo-Pacific engagement and the emerging security architecture; (d) India's naval and strategic capabilities in this region; and (e) India's future pathways and its engagement in the Asia-Pacific and Indo-Pacific. This essay endeavours to elucidate the frameworks of the Indo-Pacific, the diplomatic, economic and strategic dimensions of India's engagement and the operational contexts of its performance.

The Indo-Pacific is the new geopolitical construction that has emerged to symbolize the seamless contours of the Indian and Pacific oceans. This construction has replaced the Asia-Pacific in 2011 and has been given as a self-evident reality that has embraced the Western Pacific, the Eastern Pacific and the Eastern Indian Ocean rim. The construction has also been defined as a region that envelops a wide area from the Western Pacific to the Western Indian Ocean reaching the East African shores. The term Indo-Pacific was elucidated by the geopolitics scholar Karl Haushofer coining the term as '*Indopazifischen Raum*'. [1]

Haushofer termed it as the 'dense Indo-Pacific concentration of humanity and cultural empire of India and China, which are geographically sheltered behind the protective veil of the offshore island arcs'. During the Second World War, the term Indo-Pacific was used to connote the seamless maritime theatres of war operations by the Allied Powers. [2] Until recently, the term Asia-Pacific was used in the literature that denoted the continental and maritime littoral of this vast region. The Indo-Pacific has been a re-invention due to the high visibility and strategic footprint of the United States, China and India with their expanding economic and strategic presence and the new realignments that have been taking place.

Framework of the Indo-Pacific

The Indo-Pacific region in its evolutionary design could be debated from several perspectives. There could be seven approaches that characterize the design of the Indo-Pacific. They are as follows: (a) Constructivism of the Indo-Pacific; (b) Balance of power in the Indo-Pacific; (c) Power Shift in the Indo-Pacific; (d) Strategic autonomy choices in the region; (e) Concert of democracies in the Indo-Pacific; (f) Indo-Pacific regionalism and (g) Indo-Pacific commons.

Constructivism of the Indo-Pacific envisages that the ideas and images of the Indo-Pacific have been the construction of regionalism and geopolitics. The construction reveals the confluence of the two oceanic theatres of their profiles and competing interests. Constructivism posits the view that the Indian and Pacific Oceans present—the respective institutional and operational entities that are unique to the region—but the dynamic evolution of interests of the states in the two regions present a seamless maritime region [3] Viewed from classical geopolitics, the Indo-Pacific region represents the physical-spatial definition. The critical geopolitics dimension introduces the significance of the perceptions and ambitions of the states in the region.

Constructivism also envisages the conceptualization of the political and diplomatic dimensions of strategy and operations of the major powers in the region and the extra regional powers. Yet another dimension of constructivism is the ability to view scope of the economic dimensions of engagement of the major powers of the region.

Balance of Power in the Indo-Pacific elucidates the changing power dynamics in the region. The regional balance witnesses the emergent complexities of an emerging multi-polar balance (US, China, India, Japan, Australia and the secondary powers of East and Southeast Asia). While the United States is the dominant and resident power of the region and China is the emerging economic and strategic power, the power changes between the two major powers in the region are seen as responses to China's power rise. The US rebalancing in the region and the creation of the Asian Pivot is seen as a strategic response to China's military assertiveness and the spiralling of crisis and conflicts in the East and South China Seas. [4] A variant of the balance of power dynamics is power transition.

Power transitions between the US and China is hastening the military competition between China and US and it has increased the regional concerns of the states responding to the power rise of China. Power transition is the process that commences with the dissatisfaction of the rising powers towards the dominant overlay of the regional and global hegemon, whereby economic and security guarantees to the region could be challenged by the rising power, dissatisfied with the system. The balance of power in the Indo-Pacific has been evident in the naval and air forces modernization and the revamping of capabilities of the regional states and the extra-regional powers.

Power Shift in the Indo-Pacific is exemplified in the US rebalancing efforts that is conceptually and operationally a counter-response to the power rise of China and the arguments about the US decline. Power shift is also discussed in the context of the China's assertive rise and the strides in economic and strategic areas in the face of regional apprehensions in Southeast and East Asia. The US rebalance vis-à-vis China is bringing into focus the rejuvenation of economic and commercial interdependence of the US with the region as well as the alliances that are reinforced with its traditional allies and the new partners. [5] Power shift in effect preps the Southeast Asian states to focus on the Indo-Pacific as a means to counter-balance China with the US, Japan, India Australia and South Korea joining the dynamics. The US sponsored Trans-Pacific Partnership is the economic dimension of the US re-engagement in the region and also serves to provide the ballast to the pivot that it has been proposing and developing in the region.

Strategic Autonomy Choices in the Region features the regional perspective of how rising powers could envision their role and scope of engagement in the region. The Indian perspective of the Indo-Pacific is yet unclear even as India has a divided opinion of an expansive engagement in the Indo-Pacific even as it is incrementally engaging with the neighbourhood in Southeast Asia. While the broad consensus links the Indian and US interests in convergence for the Indo-Pacific, certain sections of the Indian strategic community views the necessity of an Indian approach to the Indo-Pacific as independent of other approaches. [6] Strategic autonomy choices entails that India could be determine by its strategic core interests of the scope and momentum of its Indo-Pacific engagement. India's expanding engagement with Japan, Australia and South Korea presents the prospect of an emergent Indo-Pacific perspective that is determined by its own interests and space of operations. On the other hand, the constricted view of India's strategic autonomy lies in the perspective that its interests would be better served through regional constructs like the ASEAN and EAS that would provide a substantial engagement. India's pivot in the Indo-Pacific emerges from the strategic partnerships it has developed with US, Japan, South Korea and the emerging partnership with Australia.

Strategic partnerships involving the US-Japan-South Korea-Australia and the India-Japan-South Korea; and India-Japan-Australia dimensions are evolving.

Concert of Democracies in the Indo-Pacific has been a

well-elucidated concept that has been employed in the contexts of unity and convergence of democracies in the region with the United States. The theme of 'concert of democracies' had been used in the World War II contexts of fighting against authoritarian governments. The concert of democracies has been employed as a norm of the US led alliance partners and friends in the region to portray and project allied interests on economic and political fronts. In the contemporary context, it has its purported employment vis-à-vis China and North Korea as an enabling tool for Japan, South Korea and Australia. Concert of democracies is employed in the context of the neo-liberal economic interdependence and the free transit and passage in the seas of the region. [7]

The post-Tsunami relief operations in 2005 under the Operation Unified Assistance drew the democratic powers of US, Japan, Australia and India into concerted maritime based humanitarian relief rehabilitation operations in the Southeast Asian region and the expanse of the Indian Ocean. The Malabar 07-02 naval exercises in 2007 involving US, India, Japan, Singapore and Australia exemplified the democracy ethos of the confluence of democratic states in the region. It had also evoked predictable and strong reactions from Beijing. Democracy and its diffusion in Asia has been a primary goal of the US and also it had engaged the same in its pursuit with India, Japan, Australia, South Korea and the countries of ASEAN.

Indo-Pacific Regionalism provides the maritime basis of the region that is based on the primacy of maritime power and trade linking the countries throughout the region. [8] It is, thus, the emergent framework of the region that has the accents of strong economic growth; growing interdependence and also features of high levels of military expenditure, leading to arms race. The regional frameworks of Indo-Pacific regionalism are built on the basis of the existing economic regional arrangements of the ASEAN, ARF, EAS, APEC and the new Trans-Pacific Partnership which is also gaining accent to undergird the economic foundations of the Indo-Pacific. Indo-Pacific regionalism also envisages the scope of US alliances in the region and its impact on India and the other countries.

Indo-Pacific Commons is yet another framework that defines the maritime commons that is formed on the linkages of the countries. The Indo-Pacific commons comprise of the sub-regions of Northeast, Southeast, and Southern Asia and the waterways of the Indian Ocean, Bay of Bengal, Straits of Malacca, South China Sea, Taiwan straits and the Pacific expanse—the 'commons' include the thousands of miles of coastline in the Indo-Pacific region, key aerial transit routes, and undersea passages and the outer space. The framework has two triangles of countries that are concentric and that have critical interests in the security and stability of the region and the tranquil transit and trade amongst them. An inner triangle of countries of Southeast Asia (Malaysia, Singapore, Indonesia, Vietnam, Philippines) that enclose the South China Sea and an outer triangle of India, South Korea, Japan and Australia that have critical interests in the stability of the region. [9]

India has been expanding its maritime profile steadily since 2001, with its growing trade with Southeast Asia, East Asia and the Pacific regions. The expanding trade profile had also witnessed the growth of its strategic capabilities— specifically its naval expansion that has come with modernisation and expanding operations. India's expansion in its 'Look East Policy' has however undergone three stages. In the late 1990s, it saw India's direction of policy with a Southeast Asia focus resulting in the consolidation of its interests; with expanding economic ties and the institutionalization of India-ASEAN engagement. It witnessed the growing economic interdependence, trade ties, diaspora connections and defence diplomacy.

The following decades saw the expansion of India's 'Look East Policy' further eastward with Japan, South Korea, Russia and the United States; even as India's economic ties swung eastward along with its strategic bilateral and multilateral exchanges. India's continued eastward focus has also been solidly based on its maritime footprint and its expanding ties, brought with it its engagement with Australia. In 2007, India was engaged in its Malabar Exercises with the US, Japan, Australia and Singapore, signifying this expanding reach. India's Maritime doctrines of 2007 and 2009 had espoused this enlargement in terms of engaging with the Pacific nations with a prominent presence in Southeast Asia. What are the defining criteria of geopolitics of the Indo-Pacific? What are India's interests in the region? How does India define it in terms of its strategic autonomy are some of the issues that need to be analyzed.

Geopolitics of the Indo-Pacific

The Indian Ocean had always been an area of strategic neglect after the British withdrawal from East of Suez in 1972, while the Pacific Ocean featured a high degree of prominence owing to the presence of the three great powers viz. United States, Soviet Union and China. The Pacific Ocean was a critical maritime basin that featured forward deployments of navies and of economic interdependence. Asia-Pacific was the common denominator of the academic and strategic literature that had a wide usage. India in its quest for its 'Look East Policy' was focused more on Asia-Pacific as a single entity for economic exchanges and interdependence.

The new vista of the Indo-Pacific has been an American invention that tended to integrate the two oceans as seamless. Secretary of State Hillary Clinton used the term to emphasize the prominence of the "Indo" in the binary concept of the Indo-Pacific. From an Indian viewpoint, it is debatable whether the politics of this term 'Indo' refers to India in the Indian Ocean context or is it an American stratagem to build coalitions that would involve India as the fulcrum in the new architecture that the US intends to build vis-à-vis China. [10] The politics of this usage has evoked some debate in India on its given stance. The issue is, should India act in its strategic autonomy to build its own conceptions of the emergent security architecture in the region or follow the great power alliances led by the US.

A second strand of the geopolitics of the region that evokes the strategic debate is the triangular strategic transactions between United States, China and India in the region. With the US hinging its strategic pivot in the region by way of deployments of its naval and air forces and the economic re-engagement in the region, it is acknowledged that the US is responding to the economic and strategic assertion of China in the region—responding to the concerns of its allies. [11] The US rebalance is also seen augmenting its resources to the region in an era of its relative decline. The Indo-Pacific geopolitical construction provides to the US, the means to bolster its presence and also engage in coalition building, strengthening the existing hub and spoke alliances with Japan, South Korea and Australia. The US also wishes to engage in strategic partnership with India to provide a hedge against China in the western flank and Japan on the eastern flank. The orchestration of the Indo-Pacific and the strategic engagement of India are seen as a catalyst to Indian proaction in the region at the US behest. India needs to assess at this juncture how its strategic interests would be promoted and to what extent its strategic autonomy would be preserved. Given India's engagement with the Pacific powers through naval diplomacy, [12] is India working for the US architecture to contain China or is India balancing its interests evenly, that needs to be assessed.

The third strand of the geopolitics of the Indo-Pacific is the oft-talked Asia Pivot. Given Asia's economic rise and the strategic competition that is now ensuing in the region, Great powers are creating their pivots in the region. The US rebalancing of its forces and the economic initiative of the Trans Pacific Partnership intends to establish a US Asia pivot. China, on the other hand, has been strengthening its economic engagement with the East Asia Summit and has been deepening its economic exchanges with Southeast Asia. [13] China's Asia pivot comes in the form of its expanding naval modernisation and the desire to expand its zone of influence and control through its second and third island chains into the Western Pacific and also into the Indian Ocean. China's disputes with Japan and its South China Sea disputes with its Southeast Asian neighbours have been marks of its expanding strategic footprint that has come out in the form of area deployments in the Indian Ocean and its strategic naval capabilities expanding in the South and East China Seas. In this context, it is essential to infer what would be the pivot that India is determined to establish and pursue. Would it be a part of the coalition building with US leadership or is India determined to pursue its autonomous interests in the region.

The fourth strand of the geopolitics of the region is the strategic proaction of the emerging powers of the region namely, Japan, South Korea and Australia. The US-led alliance ties the emerging powers with the United States in the hub and spokes model. US security guarantees with these powers is bolstered with extensive economic interdependence and trade. [14] In the face of the assertive rise of China, the emerging powers are pursuing their agendas of strategic modernization with US encouragement and support. India has growing and deepening economic exchanges with the emerging powers of the Pacific and reciprocally the emerging powers have been investing in India and have also limited forward presence in the Indian Ocean. India's economic and strategic exchanges with the emerging powers, positions India into the Indo-Pacific as part of its extended neighbourhood.

The fifth strand of the regional geopolitics is the evidence of power transition in the Indo-Pacific. Power transitions between the US and China is hastening the military competition between China and US and it has increased the regional concerns of the states responding to the power rise of China. Power transition is the process that commences with the dissatisfaction of the rising powers towards the dominant overlay of the regional and global hegemon, whose economic and security guarantees to the region could be challenged by the rising powers, dissatisfied with the system. [15] The balance of power in the Indo-Pacific has been evident in the naval and air forces modernization and the revamping of their capabilities of the regional states and the extra-regional powers.

With the above geopolitics that is evident, what are India's stakes in the region? How would India navigate the turbulence and the promise of the region that is rife with several challenges?

India's Strategic Engagement with Indo-Pacific

India's 'Look East Policy' is expanding and consolidating beyond Southeast Asia with its reach extending to Japan, South Korea and Australia. Economic exchanges and trade with the three powers have increased in a colossal manner. Similarly, India's strategic engagements with the three Pacific powers have been increasing. India's naval footprint has reached the Eastern Pacific and it has resulted in the institutionalisation of bilateral exercises with these powers.

With these developments, the moot question that is raised is, is there a niche for India in the Indo-Pacific region? This is often queried in the strategic and policy community in India and the region. India's interests could be termed in terms of the concentric layers of its presence and engagement. [16] In the near term, India's interests are in its own backyard and the Indian Ocean. This is pivotal, as its engagement in the immediate neighbourhood is vital. Given the prospects of challenges and threats from Pakistan and China in the region, India's focus has been to secure its flanks as well as work out its naval diplomacy and build in benign, its naval capacity with the smaller states in the Indian Ocean like Sri Lanka, Maldives, Seychelles and Mauritius.

Since 2001, India's economic and strategic engagement with Southeast Asia has expanded incrementally with closer interdependence and strategic partnership with several Southeast Asian states like Singapore, Vietnam, Indonesia and Philippines. India's 'Look East Policy' had incrementally expanded into East Asia following its partnerships with Japan, exemplified by its salient economic, trade and commercial partnerships. Beacuse of the NSG waiver for India, India and Japan have been closely looking into bilateral strategic partnerships and naval exercises in the East Pacific. India's engagement has also been expanding with South Korea in various areas of engagement that has resulted in greater strategic partnership between India and the East Asian powers. India's engagement with the East Asia Summit has been an important milestone as economic interdependence expands. Hence, the economic rationale for strategic partnerships has been the primary energizing source for India's expanding role in the region.

Yet another debate in the strategic community within India has been about how India should shape its eastward engagement in the context of its strategic autonomy that dictates that India should stand for its independent policy and should shun dependence on other powers or being dictated by other powers in terms of its foreign policy and security policy. There is a considerable divide in this regard as to how the Indian strategic community prefers to posture this question. However, strategic autonomy choices in the region feature the regional perspective of how rising powers could envision their role and scope of engagement in the region. The Indian perspective of the Indo-Pacific is not yet clear. There is a divided opinion over the expansive engagement in the Indo-Pacific even as it is engaging the neighbourhood in Southeast Asia. The linking of Indian and US interests are seen in the context of convergence for the Indo-Pacific. There are, however, certain sections of the Indian strategic community that view the necessity of an Indian approach to the Indo-Pacific as independent of other approaches. [17]

Even as this remains an important factor in India's engagement, there has been a steady increase in India's strategic initiatives that have come in recent years. It has been exemplified in the expansion of its naval diplomacy in the region. India's naval diplomacy and its symbolic forward presence has been the singular factor that has shaped India's

Indo-Pacific operational picture.

Five causal factors have been significant in India's Asia/Pacific and Indo-Pacific engagement.

India and the evolving Asia-Pacific security architecture presents an important challenge and opportunity. India's perception of the Asia-Pacific security architecture is now increasingly aligned with the larger canvas of Asian geopolitics of which continental geopolitics of the India-China theatre and the maritime geopolitics of the Indian and Pacific Oceans, predominate. In view of India's growing economy and rising economic interdependence, commercial and trade linkages with the Asia-Pacific including China, lies in a peaceful, stable and secure Asia-Pacific which is vital for trade and freedom of navigation in the South China Sea and East Pacific for economic and energy sea lanes of communication since they constitute the basis for India's deeper economic integration with the region. [18]

The stability of the Asia-Pacific security architecture is being induced to enormous pressure ramped by China in the South China Sea with unrelenting disputes with Vietnam and Philippines. In the East China Sea, the imposition of the Air Defence Identification Zones and the escalating tensions over the Senkaku and Diayou islands with Japan has been persistent. With India's trade and energy sea lanes of communication running from the Russian Far East Sakhalin through these turbulent waters, India has serious apprehensions of the cascading scenarios in the region.

India's responses and options have been through the diplomatic processes of engaging with ASEAN through ARF and ADMM Plus, while simultaneously energizing its Indian Ocean initiatives with Indian Ocean Rim Association and Indian Ocean Naval Symposium that could intensify engagement of Singapore, ASEAN states and East Asian powers like Japan, South Korea and Australia. This would also come with India's engagement with the Western Pacific Naval Symposium along with its economic and security diplomacy with Australia, New Zealand and the Pacific Islands Forum.

China and the Asia-Pacific security architecture: India's role and responses presents an important economic and strategic dimension of China's rise and engagement with the region. While China's assertive behaviour persists in the South China Sea and East China Sea, China has launched the Maritime Silk Road (MSR) and the Asian Infrastructure Investment Bank (AIIB) of which India, Singapore and ASEAN states are members. China's successful engagement in the Regional Comprehensive Economic Partnership (RCEP) and its ability to integrate ASEAN countries and other countries in the region speaks of its intense deeper economic engagement that would present an 'Asia only membership' to the RCEP, while elbowing the United States out. [19] On the other hand, China's continued strategic military modernization with its emphasis on its naval aerospace and missile capabilities have been building the entire array of anti-access and area denial technologies and weaponry that intends to dent the US hegemonic overlay and erode the US alliance system in the Asia-Pacific. [20]

India's role and responses have come in terms of greater security convergence with exercises, exploration of defence technology initiatives and intensifying strategic partnerships with Southeast Asia. With Singapore in the lead, India has also been able to craft strategic convergence with Japan, South Korea and Australia—with United States supporting these initiatives. Thus, India is the focus of being enmeshed in Southeast Asia and as well as the East Asia region, given the increasing economic interdependence and security convergence. [21]

The US rebalance, pivot and India's responses would factor India's role in the Asia-Pacific even as the US attempts to rebalance and establish its pivot in the Asia-Pacific. The US-led Trans Pacific Partnership (TPP) is being ambitiously driven, complimenting and competing with the Regional Comprehensive Economic Partnership (RCEP).

India's endorsement of the US rebalance and pivot has resulted in being projected as "linchpin of America's new defence strategy or rebalancing towards the Asia-Pacific". [22]

India's strategic location in the Indian Ocean Region (IOR) and its growing naval capabilities converges with the US Pacific Command's strategic interests in the Indo-Pacific over a variety of hard power issues. Given the dynamics of the US rebalance in the region to countervail China's rising presence, India, Japan and Australia join the United States in a strategic axis vis-à-vis China.

The Chinese Maritime Silk Road (MSR) and its maritime connectivity in Southeast Asia, Indian Ocean and Southern Asia has been a major concern for India and the United States. The lack of transparency of Chinese intentions and the inability to fathom the strategic implications of the project by India and the United States causes major dilemmas. [23] The vision statement of India and United States in January 2015 in Delhi U.S.-India joint strategic vision for the Asia-Pacific and Indian Ocean region intends to counter the 'One Road One Belt' of China by boosting trade connectivity and energy transmission thereby fostering free trade and people to people linkages. India and the United States strongly reiterate the freedom of navigation in the Indo-Pacific particularly in the South China Sea with emphasis for mercantile and naval vessels to be deployed in the region.

India as 'security provider' in the Asia-Pacific/Indo-Pacific is the emerging reality even as India expands its naval order of battle. India's expanding orders of battle in its armed forces, specially its navy and air force with the emphasis on amphibious and expeditionary capabilities, is increasing its capabilities, potential and performance to undertake a variety of operational missions that range from the coercive, compellance, benign and humanitarian operations within the region and beyond. [24] The "Aden to Malacca" geographical swath of area now comes within the capabilities reach of the Indian Navy. India's initiatives of the *Milan* and the Indian Ocean Naval Symposium *IONS* have accrued the institutional value addition to the prevalent ties and have fostered better naval engagement, providing India 'a naval corridor in the South China Sea all the way to the East Pacific' for engagements with Japan, South Korea, Russia and the United States.

India's maritime multilateralism with Southeast Asia and its growing profile with Japan, Australia and South Korea in East Asia is now building the potential for a stabilizing role as well as the promise of a net security provider in the sea lanes of the Indo-Pacific. India and specifically the Indian Navy has all the elements of the benign scope of building maritime security in the Asia-Pacific region.

Besides the impact of deployable forces, India's defence diplomacy burnishes the credentials of its role as a 'net security provider'. India's defence diplomacy covers a broad range of activities, including the Ministry of Defence training courses and education programmes that include military education and training opportunities for overseas military cadets and officers who attend courses at India's military training establishments. [25] It also features the loan service personnel, short-term training teams, and civilian and military advisers being deputed to foreign governments for extended periods.

India's Naval Initiatives and Extended Naval Footprint

India's maritime strategy has been evolving to a definitive Eastward focus since 2007. The release of the capstone maritime doctrine of Indian Maritime Doctrine INBR 8 (April 2004) was the basis of India's naval activism. This was followed by other statements viz., the Indian Navy's *Vision Statement* (May 2006); *Roadmap to Transformation* (October 2006). The *Freedom to Use the Seas: India's Maritime Military Strategy (IMMS)* (September 2007) was the benchmark document that provided the initial impetus of a new Indian vision of articulating its eastward focus. Several platform and infrastructure developments attribute to the growing interest of India for adding sinews to its eastern fleet that is gaining momentum with hosting and conducting fleet exercises with the Southeast Asian navies and with the Pacific powers like South Korea, Japan, United States and even Russia.

India's naval capabilities and its impact on the Indo-Pacific is an enduring salient feature that has a very crucial footprint besides the economic interdependence and growing integration. The following is the salience of this growing trend.

Anchoring benign and cooperative exercises has been the Indian Navy's role in Southeast Asia and the Indo-Pacific region has been in the accents promoting benign and cooperative maritime security. Through its naval and maritime initiatives like MILAN and Indian Ocean Naval Symposium (IONS), India's naval diplomacy and footprint have been enhanced. The Indian Navy has been hosting this endeavour since 1995 and today, more than 30 states have featured their presence and participation. MILAN had featured Australia, Indonesia, Malaysia, Myanmar, Singapore, Sri Lanka and Thailand. Besides the multilateral exercise, India has been working on bilateral maritime initiatives with Singapore, Malaysia, Thailand, Indonesia and Vietnam to augment the scope of maritime intelligence by sharing concerning transnational threats of maritime piracy and terrorism and optimizing the institutionalization of contacts. Besides MILAN, India has launched the Indian Ocean Naval Symposium (IONS) since 2008 and this has engaged the Southeast Asian nations as part of the extended Indian Ocean community.

Augmenting humanitarian and disaster response capacities: The Indian Navy was one of the first responders to the Asian Tsunami 2004 humanitarian crisis and disaster. The Indian Navy from its Andaman & Nicobar Islands Command base swung into action to extend humanitarian relief supplies to Aceh in Indonesia, Phuket in Thailand, besides assistance to Sri Lanka and Maldives. Indian Naval ships, aircraft, helicopters, and personnel responded to the Tsunami in the

Indian Ocean promptly. The Indian Navy deployed 32 naval ships, seven aircraft and 20 helicopters in support of five rescue, relief and reconstruction missions. In the concerted effort of *Operation Unified Assistance*, the Indian Navy was joined by the US Navy expeditionary strike group of the *USS Theodore Roosevelt* and the *USS Richard Bonhomie* along with the detachments of the Japanese Coast Guard and the Royal Australian Navy in the concerted humanitarian relief operations in the Thailand and Indonesia. India has been building expeditionary capabilities that would have significant capacity for playing an important role in humanitarian disaster relief. Besides, the Navy has been augmenting new platforms and capabilities for enhanced expeditionary capacity for crisis response as well as disaster response. [26]

Deployment of task forces has been a frequent event with the Eastern Fleet even as the Navy had dispatched taskforces into the South China Sea and extending it to the Pacific. The Indian Navy's Eastern Fleet has been carrying out exercises with the Japanese Maritime Self Defence Force. Enroute to the North-Eastern Pacific, the ships usually make port calls in Malaysia, Vietnam, Indonesia and Philippines. The taskforce on return journey had also embarked on exercises with the PLAN. The deployment of annual task forces to Southeast Asia and the Pacific signifies India's intent and capability to retain and sustain the economic and energy interests in the Sakhalin and the strategic stake of the Navy in the Pacific. The deployment of taskforces and the expeditionary capability reflect the Indian Navy's objective of "desired power projection force levels, influence events ashore and undertake military operations other than war". [27]

The deployment of the taskforces have been sustained with various tiers of exercises with Southeast Asian navies and the Pacific navies of South Korea, Japan, Russia and the United States, demonstrating the capacity and varied complexity of the platforms with various naval forces.

Increasing importance to interoperability: The Indian

Navy's exercises with Southeast Asian navies have varied levels of scope with the different naval forces of the regions. Indian naval operations have the objective to develop capacity for interoperability with the various Southeast Asian navies and East Asian Navies including the PLA-Navy. Although each force varies in terms of different operational capacities and platform capabilities, interoperability may not be feasible with the vast differences in training, operations and platforms, yet the exercises with each of the navies, provide the Indian Navy, familiarity of operations and development of capacity. Although the exercises cannot accrue real offensive capability, the scope of potential in terms of cooperative and constabulary elements remains high.

Expanding great power naval engagement has envisaged India to join the great power concert in Southeast Asia and Asia-Pacific with its maritime forward presence. India features as a major power along with Japan and South Korea in terms of economic and strategic engagement. India's naval engagement in the region would continue as a significant factor even as the PLA-Navy expansion and its surge into the Indian Ocean region continues. India's strategic engagement with the Southeast Asian and East Asian navies would be a counter-bulwark to the PLAN expansion in the region. Even as India expands with its naval engagements with the United States, Japan, South Korea, Russia and Australia in the Eastern Pacific as well as in the Indian Ocean region, its role as a significant actor in the region enhances its credibility.

India's gradual increase of the size and the sophistication of its warship dispatches into the region and increasing complexity of its naval exercises with Pacific powers of Japan and South Korea; its participation in the Western Pacific Naval Symposium and the enlargement of the Malabar series within Indian and the Pacific waters, burnishes India's credentials to an important benchmark of its power status.

Sustaining India's naval footprint has been a strategic priority for the Indian Navy even as new platforms have been added to the Eastern Fleet. India's nuclear submarine platforms both the Russian leased boat and the Indian vessel are deployed in the Eastern Fleet and the addition of the *INS Vikramaditya* to the Western Fleet has been operationalized. India's next aircraft carrier would join the Eastern Fleet, significantly enhancing carrier air power. With the increase of the frigates and destroyers to the fleet that comes by way of the carrier task group; it would provide the lateral platform expansion that comes along with the new combat capabilities.

Reinforcing naval basing infrastructure has been an important priority for the Navy and has a substantial resource outlays in India's defence expenditure. The commissioning of the INS Baaz in the Campbell Bay of the Andaman Nicobar Island chain, overlooking the Six Degree Channel and the Malacca Strait is an example to quote. Naval basing infrastructure could serve as important storage points for the dispensing of humanitarian and disaster relief as well as aid in the service and replenishment of the fleet ships. India's Asia/Pacific and Indo-Pacific engagement is thus salient with great potential and with growing capabilities, provides crucial stabilizing force for Southeast Asia and East Asia regional stability and balance.

India's naval strategy towards the Indo-Pacific has an ambient scope and vision with its bilateral as well as multilateral ties with all countries in the region. These ties are the catalytic basis for building enduring strategic partnerships in the Indo-Pacific maritime basin. The synchronization of India's diplomatic and strategic objectives would go along with the growing commercial-economic-energy ties that India has weaved with Southeast Asia, East Asia and the Indo-Pacific. India's build-up of naval capabilities, maritime infrastructure, closer naval partnerships and the capacity building of the Southeast Asian navies goes to build benign and cooperative partnerships between India and the region. Southeast Asia thus serves as the strategic bridge for India even as it sets its sights for the Indo-Pacific and the desire to its blue-water ambitions.

India's crucial balancing role in a prospective US-China duopoly of the Asia-Pacific regional order would serve to enhance its presence and would augur a meaningful role to its power. With the discontents of an assertive China and a dilemma ridden American power, India's role and stabilizing impact would build the sinews of strength of a regional order that is not entirely swayed to the ruthless hegemony of China nor suffer from the pangs of the US strategic dilemma of staying engaged in the region. In an obvious power transition, India's normative leadership backed by its pragmatic calculus of economic strength and strategic capacity would provide the necessary foundations of India's proaction in East Asia and the Indo-Pacific.

Endnotes

1. Ernst Haushofer, "An English Translation and Analysis of Major Karl Ernst Haushofer's Geopolitics of the Pacific Ocean", Lewis Tambs and Ernst Brehm, Lampeter: Edwin Mellor, 2002, p. 141.
2. Bruce Cumings, "Rimspeak; or the Discourse of the Pacific Rim", in ArifDirlik (ed.), 'What is in a Rim?: Critical Perspectives on the Pacific Region Idea', Oxford: Rowman & Littlefield, 1998, pp. 53-72.
3. David Scott, "The Indo-Pacific: New Regional Formulations and New Maritime Frameworks for US-India Strategic Convergence", *Asia-Pacific Review*, Vol. 19, No. 2, 2012, p. 86.
4. John Bradford, "The Maritime Strategy of the United States: Implications for Indo-Pacific Sealanes", *Contemporary Southeast Asia*, Vol. 33, No. 2, August 2011.
5. Michael Auslin, "Getting it Right, Japan and Trans-Pacific Partnership", *Asia-Pacific Review,* Vol. 19, Issue 1, 2012, pp. 23-24.
6. Priya Chacko, "India and the Indo-Pacific: An Emerging Regional Vision", *Policy Brief*, Issue 5, November 2012, Indo-Pacific Governance Research Centre, Adelaide.
7. C. Raja Mohan, "Great Powers and Asia's Destiny: A View from Delhi", *Political Science*, December 2012, Vol. 64, No. 2.

8. Dennis Rumley, Timothy Doyle and Sanjay Chaturvedi, "Securing the Indian Ocean? Competing Regional Security Constructions", *Policy Brief,* Issue 3, April 2012, Indo-Pacific Governance Research Centre, Adelaide.
9. Michael Auslin, "Security in the Indo-Pacific Commons: Toward a Regional Strategy", Washington DC: American Enterprise Institute, December 2010, accessed at: http://www.aei.org/papers/foreign-and-defense-policy/regional/asia/security-in-the-indo-pacific-commons.
10. For a very detailed analysis, see Priya Chacko (2014), "The Rise of the Indo-Pacific: Understanding Ideational Change and Continuity in India's Foreign Policy", *Australian Journal of International Affairs*, Vol. 68, No. 4, pp. 432-454, DOI:10.1080/10357718.2014.891565; C. Raja Mohan (2013), "India: Between Strategic Autonomy and Geopolitical Opportunity", *Asia Policy*, No. 15, January 2013, Seattle, WA; National Bureau of Asia Research, pp. 21-25, 10.1353/asp.2013.0006.
11. Rory Metcalf elaborates the emergent dynamics of US alliances and the emerging US-China economic and strategic dynamics in, "Reimagining Asia: From Asia-Pacific to Indo-Pacific", *Open Forum, The Asan Forum,* January-February 2016, Vol. 4, No. 1. See, Mohan Malik (ed.), 'Maritime Security in the Indo-Pacific: Perspectives from China, India and the United States', Lanham, MD: Rowman and Littlefield, 2014. For a robust interesting Indian perspective, see, Vivek Mishra (2016), "US Power and Influence in the Asia-Pacific Region: The Decline of Alliance Mutuality", *Strategic Analysis*, DOI: 10.1080/09700161.2016.1156251.
12. David Scott (2012), "India and the Allure of the Indo-Pacific", *International Studies,* Vol. 49, Nos. 3 & 4, pp. 1-24.
13. For a good survey of analysis, see, David Lampton, "A New Type of Major-Power Relationship: Seeking a Durable Foundation for U.S-China Ties", *Asia Policy,* Essay No. 16, July 2013, accessed at: http://www.nbr.org/publications/element.aspx?id=650; Michael Evans, "Power and Paradox: Asian Geopolitics and Sino-American Relations in the 21st Century," *Orbis,* Winter 2011, p. 112 and David Shambaugh, "A Big Step Forward in US-China Relations", accessed at:

http://www.chinausfocus.com/foreign-policy/a-big-step-forward-in-u-s-china-relations/.

14. A good analysis is by Metcalf and Raja Mohan in Rory Medcalf and C. Raja Mohan (2014), "Responding to Indo-Pacific Rivalry: Australia, India and Middle Power Coalitions", Sydney: Lowry Institute for International Policy, August, accessed at: http://www.lowyinstitute.org/files/responding_to_indo-pacific_rivalry_0.pdf.
15. For a good analysis, see Alexander L. Vuwing (2012), "The Future of China's Rise: How China's Economic Growth Will Shift the Sino-US Balance of Power: 2010-2040", *Asian Politics and Policy,* Vol. 4, No. 3; pp. 401-423; and Liu Mingfu, "The China Dream: The Great Power Thinking and Strategic Positioning of China in the Post-American Age", New York, CN, Time Books and William A. Callahan, "China's Strategic Futures: Debating the Post-American World Order", *Asian Survey*, Vol. 52, No. 4, 2012, pp. 634-635.
16. "India's Evolving Security Relations and Partnerships in the Indo-Pacific", in David Michel and Ricky Paserelli (2014) (eds.) 'Sea Change: Maritime Geopolitics in the Indo-Pacific Region', Washington DC: The Henry Stimson Centre, December accessed at: http://www.stimson.org/images/uploads/research-pdfs/SEA-CHANGE-WEB.pdf.
17. Harsh V. Pant (2013), "Looking East: India's Growing Role in Asian Security", *Commentary*, Seattle: WA., National Bureau of Asian Research, accessed at: http://www.nbr.org/downloads/pdfs/outreach/NBR_IndiaCaucus_Sept2013.pdf and Priya Chacko (2013), "India and the Indo-Pacific: Three Approaches", *The Strategist*, The Australia Strategic Policy Institute Blog ASPI 24, January 2013, accessed at: http://www.aspistrategist.org.au/india-and-the-indo-pacific.
18. David Scott (2012), "The Indo-Pacific: New Regional Formulations and New Maritime Frameworks for India-US Strategic Convergence", *Asia-Pacific Review* Vol. 19, Issue 2, 2012, pp. 85-109.
19. Amitendu Palit, "Trans-Pacific Partnership: India and South Asia, ISAS Insights No. 284, July 11, 2015, accessed at: http://www.isn.ethz.ch/Digital-

Library/Publications/Detail/?ots783=0c54e3b3-1e9c-be1e-2c24-a6a8c7060233&lng=en&id=192468.

20. Malcolm Cook, Raoul Heinrichs, Rory Medcalf and Andrew Shearer (2010), "Power and Choice: Asian Security Futures", Sydney: Lowy Institute for International Policy.
21. A good analysis is in Rory Medcalf and C. Raja Mohan (2014), "Responding to Indo-Pacific Rivalry: Australia, India and Middle Power Coalitions", Sydney: Lowry Institute for International Policy, August, accessed at: http://www.lowyinstitute.org/files/responding_to_indo-pacific_rivalry_0.pdf.
22. Peter A Petrie and Michael Plummer (2014), "The Trans-Pacific Partnership and Asia-Pacific Integration: Policy Implications", *Policy Brief,* Nos. 12-16, Washington DC: Peterson Institute of International Economics, accessed at: http://www.iie.com/publications/pb/pb12-16.pdf.
23. Denyer, Simon (2014), "China Promotes Asia-Pacific Dream to Counter US Pivot", *The Washington Post,* November 11, 2014, accessed at: http://www.washingtonpost.com/world/chinas-promotes-asia-pacific-dream-to-counter-us-pivot/2014/11/11/1d9e05a4-1e8e-4026-ad5a-5919f8c0de8a_story.html.
24. Lawrence Prabhakar Williams (2013), "India's Extended Maritime Mandala: Naval Intent and Strategy in Southeast Asia" in Ajaya K. Das (2013), 'India-ASEAN Defence Relations', RSIS Monograph No. 28, Singapore: S. Rajaratnam School of International Studies, accessed at: http://www.rsis.edu.sg/wp-content/uploads/2014/07/Monograph2813.pdf.
25. Arvind Dutta (2009), "Role of India's Defence Cooperation Initiatives in Meeting the Foreign Policy Goals", *Journal of Defence Studies*, Vol. 3, No. 3, July, accessed at: http://www.idsa.in/system/files/jds_3_3_adutta.pdf.
26. Abhijit Singh, "The Indian Navy's New Expeditionary Outlook", ORF Occasional Paper # 37, October 2012, New Delhi: Observer Research Foundation, accessed at: http://www.orfonline.org/wp-content/uploads/2012/10/OccasionalPaper_37.pdf.
27. "12th Defence Plan: Focus on Navy's 'Expeditionary' Ops", *The Indian Express*, May 4, 2012, accessed at:

http://www.indianexpress.com/news/12th-defence-plan-focuson-navy-s--expeditionary--ops/945283.

3

India-Pakistan Relations under Modi-led NDA Government

Sanjay K. Jha

Introduction

During campaign and after the victory of Narendra Modi-led National Democratic Alliance (NDA) in Parliamentary elections in 2014, expectation was that foreign policy would not feature prominently on the agenda of the newly elected government. It was expected that domestic priorities would dominate the agenda of the newly elected government. However, the experience since May 2014 has demonstrated that foreign policy has been one of the major highlights of the government. Strong leadership, personality factor, good chemistry with world leaders and a focus on immediate and extended neighbourhood have been interpreted as a success of foreign policy initiatives under the leadership of Narendra Modi. Many foreign policy experts have interpreted his foreign policy as a major shift from the previous United Progressive Alliance (UPA) government, led by Dr. Manmohan Singh.

With regard to Pakistan, Prime Minister Narendra Modi's decision to invite Pakistani Prime Minister Nawaz Sharif to his swearing-in ceremony on May 26, 2014, along with all other heads of states/governments from the South Asian Association for Regional Cooperation (SAARC) was interpreted by many foreign policy analysts as a 'bold step' and a decisive shift in Pakistan policy of the newly elected Narendra Modi-led government. It was hoped that the new government with a massive mandate and strong leadership is in a better position to steer relationship towards an era of constructive engagement.

However, the trajectory of India-Pakistan relationship since May 2014 has raised several questions? Have the initiatives of Narendra Modi-led government been a part of well thought out strategy or a compromise on the firm stand taken by the government that engagement with Pakistan could only be resumed if Pakistan desisted from involvement of terrorist activities directed against India. Though it would be premature at this juncture to make a definite assessment of Government of India's Pakistan policy, two distinct themes are being discussed by academics and foreign policy analysts. First, whether the government has been trying to re-define its Pakistan policy or is it simply continuing with the policy of UPA government, marked with inconsistency and lack of coherence.

This paper makes an attempt to map the contours of emerging India-Pakistan relations, particularly since the installation of Narendra Modi-led NDA government. Over the years, the core of India-Pakistan relations have been conditioned by two distinct yet inter-related themes: terrorism and Jammu and Kashmir. At the core of India's Pakistan policy has been to encourage, persuade or at times force a shift in Pakistan's policy towards terrorism and Kashmir and the principal instrument, on most of the occasions, employed for this has been dialogue and negotiation. An assessment of this framework would be useful for any attempt to analyse Pakistan policy of the current regime. Has the time come to revisit this policy framework? Has the government been trying to evolve a new framework to engage Pakistan and address issues emanating from Pakistan's approach towards issues relating to terrorism and Kashmir?

The paper seeks to advance the argument that there is a need to have a consistent approach in dealing with intractable issues with Pakistan and that approach must necessarily take into account the sources of India's policy within Pakistani state structure. Though a number of factors such as regional security dynamics, US-Pakistan relationship, evolving security architecture in Afghanistan, sustained campaign by small but vocal peace constituency within Pakistan have influenced Pakistan's foreign policy in varying degrees, the core of its policy towards India emanates from the very structure of its state, its ideology, identity and distribution of power between civil and military establishments. Even though, occasionally, the democratically elected governments in Pakistan favour better relationship with India, the overall outcomes have been shaped by the core thrust of its military establishment, which is manifested in its stand on terrorism and Kashmir.

The paper has been organized in four parts: the first part offers some introductory remarks setting the tone of the arguments presented in the paper. The second part of the chapter makes an attempt to understand foreign policy framework of the government; the third part analyses recent trends in India-Pakistan relations within that framework and argues that there has been a broad continuity in government's approach to relationship with Pakistan. The fourth part seeks to analyse options before India. And finally, some tentative conclusions have been drawn on the basis of available facts and their analysis.

Foreign Policy Objectives of the NDA Government

At the outset, it would be useful to examine as to whether the Narendra Modi-led government's Pakistan policy flows out of a well thought out strategy to pursue a proactive policy aimed towards achieving some tangible results through a series of initiatives since May 2014. Though it would be premature, at this juncture, to assess the impact of the 'pro-active policy' in terms of tangible achievement, some broad parameters can be discerned from Bhartiya Janata Party's election manifesto, public pronouncements of leader before and during election campaign of 2014 Parliamentary elections and statement from the government.

The party manifesto for 2014 elections says, "BJP believes a resurgent India must get its rightful place in the comity of nations and international institutions. The vision is to fundamentally reboot and reorient the foreign policy goals, content and process, in a manner that locates India's global strategic engagement in a new paradigm and on a wider canvass, that is not just limited to political diplomacy, but also includes our economic, scientific, cultural, political and security interests, both regional and global, on the principles of equality and mutuality, so that it leads to an economically stronger India, and its voice is heard in the international fora". [1]

Clearly, the BJP advocated for a new paradigm for foreign policy. This new paradigm flows from party's strategic vision about India's role in international order and an assessment of previous UPA government's approach to foreign policy, which in the party's view lacked strategic vision. Reiterating its commitment to 'proactive and innovative foreign policy', the resolution passed in the BJP National Executive Meeting at Bengaluru on April 3, 2015, provides a framework to understand foreign policy of the new government. The resolution says that, "The Prime Minister has pursued a bold, proactive and innovative foreign policy that is aligned with our Government's primary goal of accelerating national economic development; and to fulfil Bharat's global responsibilities as the world's most populous youth nation and largest democracy. *Samman*—dignity and honour; *Samvad*—greater engagement and dialogue; *Samriddhi*—shared prosperity; *Suraksha*—regional and global security; and *Sanskriti evam Sabhyata*—cultural and civilizational linkages; these five themes have become the *Panchamrit*—new pillars of our foreign policy". [2]

The key drivers of these initiatives have been strong leadership, more effective personal appeal of Prime Minister and his ability to strike great chemistry with leaders. In the assessment of the BJP and newly elected government, the Pakistan policy of the Manmohan Sing-led UPA government was marked with inconsistency, incoherence and lack of strategic vision. The BJP-led government said that though it would pursue friendly relations with neighbouring countries, it will not hesitate from taking "strong stand and steps". [3] Regarding cross-border terrorism, the government noted that it would deal with incursions "with a firm hand". On the issue of Kashmir, the assertion was that it won't be conciliatory to Pakistani interests and will maintain the region as "an integral part of the Union of India". There was no mention of the Composite Dialogue Process between India and Pakistan in the Election Manifesto of BJP. [4]

There was a clear indication that there will be a substantial departure in thrust and substance of government's approach towards Pakistan. Has there been a major shift in the foreign policy during NDA regime? Literature on international relations and foreign policy inform us that foreign policy of any country has broad continuity, because it is driven by national interests irrespective of change in the regime. Any major change is largely due to major shift in international system in terms of changing power-relationship between states or significant distribution of capability or major shift in domestic politics of the country. For example, after the Second World War, alignment of power at international level caused major shift in foreign policy priorities of major countries; the same happened after the end of the Cold War.

In the case of India also, the broad orientation of foreign policy was tuned to align India's interests in the changing geo-strategic environment after the end of the Cold War and collapse of bipolar world. In the case of current government also, all available evidence in the public domain indicate that there has been a broad continuity in foreign policy on major parameters irrespective of election manifesto or public pronouncements of political leaders.

India-Pakistan Relations: A Saga of Ups and Downs

When it became obvious that Narendra Modi would become Prime Minister, the question was whether the new government would continue with the policy of the previous

UPA regime or embrace a more hawkish approach towards Pakistan through some bold initiatives. All along, the BJP and Narendra Modi advocated tough action against Pakistan-sponsored terrorism and zero-tolerance towards terrorism.

However, his decision to invite Nawaz Sharif to his swearing-in ceremony on May 26, 2014, along with all other heads of states/governments from the SAARC, surprised many. The move was interpreted by many as a decisive shift in Pakistan's policy of the new NDA-led government. It was hoped that the friendly gesture by the new government with a massive mandate and strong leadership, would steer the relationship with Pakistan towards an era of constructive engagement. Available evidence suggests that there was broad consensus among Pakistan's major political formations that Nawaz Sharif should accept invitation aimed towards normalizing relationship with India. Media reports suggested that the decision by Nawaz Sharif to attend swearing-in-ceremony came after his brother and Punjab Chief Minister, Shahbaz Sharif met Army Chief General Raheel Sharif and conveyed to him the importance of the visit of India for maintaining good relationship between the two countries and peace in the region. [5]

However, the subsequent events led to a debate on the trajectory, substance and coherence of government's Pakistan policy. It may, in this context, be recalled that in August 2014, the government called off scheduled talks between Foreign Secretaries over the Pakistan High Commissioner's meeting with the leaders of All Party Hurriyat Conference (APHC) days before the dialogue. Indian government officials maintained that the invitation to Hurriyat leaders is part of a series of 'provocations' from the Pakistani government to push India into calling off talks. Speaking to media persons, the Ministry of External Affairs spokesperson said, "There is a red line we have drawn...We have told Pakistan—you either talk to us, or to them [Kashmiri separatists]". [6]

The change in the position of Government of India drew

criticism not only from opposition parties but also from foreign policy analysts. The move indicated the lack of a proper roadmap and coherence in the policy matters. Pakistan has been maintaining that APHC are the real representatives of Jammu and Kashmir and in the past also there has been a practice to consult them, as stakeholder, in negotiations with India. This, together with Pakistan's repeated violations of the 2003 ceasefire agreement and its continued support of terrorist activities against India, induced the government to make it clear that a resumption of talks was contingent on the cessation of such activities by Pakistan. [7]

However, a series of subsequent developments indicated mellowing down of the tough stand on dialogue with Pakistan. The visit of Indian Foreign Secretary, S. Jaishankar to Pakistan in March 2015 as part of his 'SAARC Yatra' was seen as a direct outreach to Pakistan towards resumption of dialogue. Further, on July 10, 2015, Narendra Modi met Nawaz Sharif on the sidelines of the SCO Summit in Ufa. They agreed that India and Pakistan have a collective responsibility to ensure peace and promote development. It was agreed that, apart from other levels of engagements, the National Security Advisor (NSA) of both the countries will meet in Delhi to discuss terrorism. However, the NSA level meeting scheduled to be held on August 23, 2015 had to be called off at the last moment due to serious disagreement on interpretation of Ufa declaration and scheduled meeting of Pakistan's NSA with Hurriyat leaders ahead of the meeting.

The proposed meeting between security advisors of both the countries was a bold step, supposedly aimed at determining a roadmap for the future of both the countries. However, it was expected that issues pertaining to interpretation of joint statement, possibility of discussion on Kashmir, Pakistan's engagement with Hurriyat leaders could have been foreseen and sufficient groundwork should have been done to avoid any last minute glitches. Yet, the government's position on the issue remained obscure almost to the time of the external affairs minister's last-minute ultimatum. [8]

Subsequently, more than four-and-a half months after the Ufa meeting, both Prime Ministers met briefly in Paris on November 30, 2015 at the Climate Change Conference. This 'pull-aside meeting' once again, set the tone for resumption of dialogue between the two countries. On December 6, 2015, NSA of both the countries met in Bangkok in a 'cordial and constructive atmosphere' and discussed peace and security, terrorism and Jammu and Kashmir. Subsequently, Indian External Affairs Minister, Sushma Swaraj visited Pakistan to attend the ministerial segment on Afghanistan during the annual Heart of Asia conference on December 9, 2015. During her visit, she met Pakistani leaders including Prime Minister Nawaz Sharif. This meeting signalled resumption of composite dialogue with Pakistan under a different nomenclature to discuss all outstanding issues between the two countries, including terrorism and Jammu and Kashmir.

The momentum was given a further push by Prime Minister Narendra Modi during his brief visit to Pakistan and his meeting with his Pakistani counterpart Nawaz Sharif on December 25, 2015. This initiative was received both by academicians and policy analysts, with a mix of optimism, surprise and scepticism. While on the one hand, the initiative has been hailed as a bold step, personal diplomacy and 'out of box thinking' to take forward relationship with Pakistan on a firm track, it has been criticized by many for inconsistency, incoherence and unilateral gesture without any assurance from Pakistan on concrete steps to address India's concerns.

Pathankot Attacks

The optimism created, once again, by Prime Minister's Lahore visit evaporated within a week when, on January 2, 2016, a group of heavily armed Pakistan-based terrorists attacked the Pathankot Air Force station in Punjab and part of the Western Air Command of the Indian Air Force. Four terrorists, one Air Force commando and two Defence Service

Core (DSC) jawans were killed in the incident. The encounter and search operation lasted for many days. Evidence collected by Indian security agencies pointed to the fact that the terrorists belonged to Pakistan-based Jaish-e-Muhammand (JeM), designated a terrorist organization by India, the US, the UK and the UN. [9] Maulana Masood Azhar, chief of JeM, and his brother Abdul Rauf Asghar, mastermind of IC-814 hijack case, are among the four persons that have been identified by the Government of India as 'handlers' behind the attack.

The Pathankot attacks can be seen in the series of terrorist attacks at a time when attempts by Government of India to improve relationship with Pakistan had evoked this kind of a response. For example, the Lahore Bus Yatra was followed by the Kargil incursions in 1999. The unsuccessful Agra Summit meeting with the then Pakistani President, General Parvez Musharraf was followed by the attack on Indian Parliament in December 2001. When the peace initiatives between Dr. Manmohan Singh and Parvez Musharraf ran into rough weather, Mumbai witnessed serial bomb blasts in trains and coordinated terrorist attacks in November 2008. Similarly, after the Ufa meetings between Narendra Modi and Nawaz Sharif, there was a terrorist attacks in Gurdaspur. [10]

It is not surprising, therefore, that despite initial assurances given by Pakistani authorities to take firm and decisive steps against perpetrators and masterminds of Pathankot attacks, nothing concrete moved on the ground. After the terrorist attacks in Pathankot, the details of terrorists, evidence of their being Pakistani, their networks etc. were shared with Pakistan at the highest level.

After the attacks, there was communication between Prime Ministers and NSAs of both the countries. There was explicit assurance from Pakistan that based on evidence provided by India, effective step will be taken to bring perpetrators and masterminds of Pathankot attacks to justice. India even allowed a five member Pakistani Joint Investigation Team

(JIT) to visit Pathankot in March 2016. The JIT interacted with Indian officials investigating the terrorist attacks and witnesses. The Indian government pressed for stern action against them as a condition for any future talks with Pakistan. But Pakistani team was not apparently satisfied with the evidence produced by India. Moreover, the Indian request to allow Indian investigators from NIA access to JeM leaders in Pakistan has not been accepted by Pakistani authorities. The reasons for Pakistani behaviour are not difficult to understand if we examine available facts and opinions of experts and analysts, who have tracked the issue.

Available facts suggest that the Pathankot attacks were masterminded by Pakistani security establishment in order to derail the peace process. Some of the media reports suggested that the attacks were masterminded by elements within the Pakistani security establishment. The six terrorists who infiltrated into India through Gurdaspur border were trained for six months at a terror camp in Bahawalpur, Pakistan. They were associated with al-Rahman trust. They were in touch with their handlers Maulana Ashfaq Ahmed and Haji Abdul Shakoor ever since they entered the Indian territory. [11] Further, media reports claimed that Indian agencies investigating the Pathankot attacks have specific lead on ISI's role in the Pathankot attacks. The report further claimed that the ISI provided logistical support, including training to terrorists, before they were launched for the fidayeen attack. [12]

US-based security expert, Christine Fair states that the Pakistan Army has launched the JeM to this attack to probe Modi government's red lines. Iit is a manifestation of Pakistan's national security strategy to pursue its revisionist agenda against India. She says, "It was a way to draw back the defected groups of JeM who had turned against the Pakistani State after President Musharraf's U-turn in 2001 and direct them against India. The attack on the air base is not a spontaneous response to recent developments. It is simply the latest manifestation of the Pakistani national security strategy to pursue its revisionist agenda against India". [13]

Another US-based expert and former White House official Bruce Riedel said that the Pathankot attack was masterminded by ISI in order to prevent détente between India and Pakistan after 'Prime Minister Narendra Modi's surprise Christmas day visit to Lahore. Riedel added that the JeM has received training and weapons from the ISI and worked closely with Al-Qaeda. [14] Riedel said that the "ISI is under the generals' command and is composed of army officers, so the spies are controlled by the Pakistani army, which justifies its large budget and nuclear weapons program by citing the Indian menace". [15]

Though it would be premature at this juncture to confirm these reports with fair amount of certainty, available evidence suggests certain amount of uneasiness within Pakistani security establishment over the prospects of improving relationship with India.

This factor, even if indicative in nature, needs to be factored in any initiative for dialogue with Pakistan. There is a constituency within India and Pakistan, who are unable or unwilling to see the peace process beyond the initiatives taken by top leaders in both the countries. The question that needs to be probed is why have the successive attempts over the years failed to achieve tangible results? To what extent have, based on experience, Pakistani security establishment reconciled to the idea of peaceful co-existence with India? What incentives will the improved relationship with India, accrue to Pakistani Army? Has the formula of formula is 'terror till you talk' and 'terror again if you stop talking', been working effectively. [16]

Pakistani State: Sources of India Policy

Developments in bilateral relationship since May 2014 have demonstrated that the Indian efforts towards improving relationship have not been matched with similar reciprocity from the Pakistani side. Right since invitation to Pakistani Prime Minister Nawaz Sharif to the swearing-in ceremony in May 2014 to the visit of Indian Prime Minister to Lahore in

December 2015, the Indian government made several efforts to break the logjam and reach out to Pakistani side. Amidst criticism within India and scepticism over unilateral gestures, the Indian Prime Minister took enormous risk with the hope that the steps taken by India will create a conducive environment to take the relationship further. The assumption has been that the democratically elected government in Pakistan under the leadership of Nawaz Sharif, on more than one occasion, indicated that it is serious about improving relationship with India. In addition, there is growing yearning for peace in civil society groups in both the countries and Pakistan will respond to peace constituency, which for long has been advocating better relationship with India.

There was also hope that Pakistan, itself a victim of terrorism, will realise that time has come to re-visit its stand on terrorism through measures that addresses concerns of India as well. In India also, there is a peace constituency that feels that Pakistan itself is a victim of terrorism and gradually the Pakistani state is realizing that there should be zero tolerance towards terrorism. In recent past, a number of steps have been taken by Pakistani authorities to address the issue of internal terrorism in the country. However, the same amount of alertness and toughness has not been demonstrated against groups operating from Pakistani soil against India. The example is slow progress in Mumbai attack case, vacillation in Pathankot case and recent episode on Masood Azhar where China blocked in UN, the proposal forwarded by India to declare Masood Azhar as a designated terrorist.

Therefore, not much appears to have changed on the ground. Over the years, Pakistan has been consistent in its approach towards India and that approach derives its sanction from its very state structure, ideology of the state, civil-military relations, distribution of power within state structure and use of extremist Islamist groups as strategic asset and as an instrument of foreign policy. The core of this strategy has been to employ terror as a tool and Islamist militant groups as strategic asset and forcing India to talk with Kashmir as a core issue. And this strategy has been successful. The security establishment in Pakistan has been confident that India will not respond militarily to Pakistan because it has been successful in internationalizing the bilateral relations through periodically talking about the low Pakistani nuclear threshold, where nuclear weapon is not just a deterrent against but actually usable against India. Pakistan army has been the chief architect of this policy.

Frederic Grare argues that given the dysfunctional civil-military relations in Pakistan and role of the army in its polity, the initiative is with Pakistan and India is left in an essentially reactive role. Therefore, even though Pakistan may officially favour better relationship with India, its security establishment and part of political establishment remain divided on the issue of terrorism, Kashmir and relationship with India. [17] The military has a substantial say on foreign policy issues, particularly with regard to relationship with India even when civilian government is in power. He says, "India, recognizing that the ball is squarely in Pakistan's court, is therefore likely to adopt a "wait and see" attitude. But New Delhi will have to walk a fine line between ignoring Pakistan (which it cannot really afford to do) and keeping the door to better relations open wide enough to provide a real incentive for Islamabad to adopt meaningful new policies—all without making unilateral concessions to Pakistan". [18]

The Army derives its legitimacy and projects a predominant role from the very ideology of state. In an interview in 1981, the then President, General Zia ul-Haq had said, "Pakistan is like Israel, an ideological state...Take out the Judaism from Israel and it will fall like a house of cards. Take Islam out of Pakistan and make it a secular state; it would collapse". [19] General Musharraf also often said that the Army of Pakistan has the responsibility of protecting the ideological frontiers of Pakistan. Developing the same ideological basis of Pakistani state, Faisal Devji, in his book

Muslim Zion: Pakistan as a Political Idea, argues that Pakistan bears a close resemblance to Israel; both nations were created amidst the decline of the British Empire, they ostensibly represented homelands for minorities fleeing real and perceived persecution, and they came into being with the transfer of large populations into territories that had previously not been inhabited by them. [20] The book further argues that Pakistan's nationalism is founded on negation coupled with religion: rejecting old land for new—dismissing Hindu India for Muslim Pakistan. Therefore, "for Muslim nationalism, religion was conceived of not as a supplement to geography but as an alternative". [21]

Sumit Ganguly analyses this ideological underpinning of Pakistani state, "...two nations remain mired in conflict due to inherent features of their nationalist agendas. Indian nationalist leadership chose to hold on to this Muslim-majority state to prove that minorities could thrive in a plural, secular polity. Pakistani nationalists argued with equal force that they could not part with Kashmir as part of the homeland created for the Muslims of South Asia". [22]

The entire edifice of Pakistani army has been built, right since the beginning, on the notion of India as their principal enemy. This ideology is deeply entrenched in its structure, orientation and training of its officials. Therefore, even though Kashmir remains the core issue in public pronouncements, the agenda is not limited to Kashmir but in preventing India's inevitable ascendance in South Asia and beyond. C. Christine Fair argues, "The country's administration (read its army), has shown unwavering resolve in protecting its Islamic ideology. But in reality, from the demand underlying the two nation theory to the country's ideological outlook and its changing nuclear weapons posture, all are aimed at one goal: parity in every respect with India, however unrealistic that goal may be". [23]

The use of extremist Islamist infrastructure, which it has created and nurtured for years and existence of nuclear weapons are critical components of this strategy. Religious extremism and gradual radicalization of part of civil society and state institutions, including Army have provided a support structure within Pakistan, which enables the Army to pursue this strategy without much opposition from within. The Islamist militant groups gives a window for deniability after every major terrorist attacks against India and nuclear weapons enable this risk-taking against India with the assumption that such activities will go unpunished.

In case of any possible escalation, the existence of nuclear weapons, will prompt US and other international powers to intervene to prevent any escalation leading to possible nuclear exchange. Pakistan's refusal to agree to a no-first use of nuclear weapons, its development of tactical nuclear weapons and its refusal to sign the Fissile Materials Cut-off Treaty indicate that its nuclear strategy has been structured around this core strategy against India. Thus, a friendly relationship with India is a threat to the Army as this institution will become irrelevant and they would face the prospect of downsizing of their strength and reduction of budgetary support. [24]

Thus, the optimism for a breakthrough is misplaced for several reasons. First, Nawaz Sharif does not hold any lever of power that matters. Even if Nawaz Sharif wants peace himself—a questionable assertion—he is not the Sharif that matters. Pakistan's Army Chief is the one in charge. Pakistan's army does not have any incentive to normalize relationship with India; rather it wants to protect its pre-eminent hold upon the state, its resources and its people, all of which is predicated upon an interminable, civilizational war with 'Hindu India'.

Debating Options before India

It is not surprising, therefore, that attempts to create positive atmosphere through various initiatives by the current government, for a positive environment for peace and dialogue, have not yielded the desired results. All available evidence indicates that the terrorist infrastructure operating from Pakistani soil are active and there has not been any concrete action by Pakistan to address key concerns of India, including arrest of prosecution of perpetrators of terrorist attacks in Mumbai and Pathankot. In this scenario, we cannot escape the fact that terrorist violence may/will continue as one of the principal tools for terrorists and their supporters, mostly based in Pakistan.

What options does India have in this situation? We have found that the Government of India has been constraint to exercise the only option of dialogue and negotiation, despite no visible change in Pakistan's attitude towards India and terrorist attacks emanating from Pakistani soil at regular intervals. This has been happening despite consistent stand taken by successive Indian governments and major political parties, after every major terrorist attacks, that terror and talks cannot go together and there will be zero tolerance towards terrorism. Even a cursory glance at the government response to major terrorist attacks would reveal that there is definite pattern of suspension and resumption of dialogue.

Whenever terrorist attacks occur, there is intense pressure on the government to suspend talks and take some steps in retaliation. Military options, surgical strike, covert operations against Pakistan, tough measures are some of the options that have been discussed in the past after every major terrorist attacks. Although these options have been seldom exercised by the government and dialogue process is resumed.

However, On September 29, 2016, eleven days after the Uri attack, the Indian army conducted "surgical strikes" against suspected militants in Pakistani-administered Kashmir.

Every time, after a few step forward, some major breakthrough is expected and one terrorist attacks brings the entire process to square one and the government.policy is criticized for not having coherence and a strategic roadmap to address bilateral relationship with Pakistan.

Experience in the past has demonstrated that India has limited options even for responding to major terrorist attacks.

For India, the primary option is to create sufficient incentives for Pakistan to abandon the path using terrorist organisations as strategic assets. The nature of Pakistani state structure and ideological moorings makes any sustained effort through negotiations a difficult option. India is therefore, condemned to remain essentially reactive until Pakistan addresses the tension in its foreign policy. On its part, India can exercise the option of resuming or suspending the peace process. As far as other options are concerned, India has very limited option, including coercing Pakistan for any favourable outcome. [25]

Coercive options, including military strikes have been debated in the past, but have not been exercised possibly due to uncertainty about tangible outcomes and costs involved. Security experts have debated a range of military and other coercive options including surgical strikes on terrorist camps, covert operations against Pakistan, coercive diplomacy, mobilizing international support against Pakistan and so on. All of these options have their associated risks. India tried coercive diplomacy through mobilization of forces along borders in the aftermath of terrorist attack on the Parliament. The military mobilization, named *Operation Parakram,* between December 2001 and October 2002 was aimed at compelling Pakistan to stop cross-border terrorism and abandon it as an instrument of foreign policy against India. [26] The exercise could not achieve its stated objectives. According to S. Kalyanraman, the reasons were "Pakistan's high stakes in Kashmir, India's lack of adequate leverage to exert greater international pressure on Islamabad, inexplicable expansion in Indian objectives and the resultant introduction of a competitive element into the equation, the non-calibrated nature of the measures adopted and needless persistence with the mobilization". [27]

Option of limited strikes on terrorist infrastructure across the LoC has been discussed in the past. In an interview to media persons, former Pakistan Foreign Minister Khurshid Mahmood Kasuri claimed on the basis of information received from US officials that in the aftermath of 26/11 terror attacks in Mumbai, India contemplated the option of carrying out surgical air strikes at the headquarters of terror outfits Jamaat-ud-Dawa (JuD) and Lashkar-e-Taiba (LeT) near Lahore. [28] The Indian government has not confirmed this and we do not have sufficient information in public domain to corroborate this claim. Still, the option of surgical strike against Pakistan has been debated by security experts and most of them have agreed that it remains uncertain whether this option would produce meaningful results and they carry a high risk of escalation up to and including the use of nuclear weapons.

Speaking to media persons in October 2014, the then National Security Advisor of Pakistan Sartaj Aziz said that India cannot afford to carry out surgical strike inside the country as it is aware of Pakistan's response to any such action. He said, "our army is fully alert and capable of appropriate response". [29] Many experts have outlined the limitations of this approach in the context of India-Pakistan relations. [30] Apart from military costs and possibility of escalation, such exercise runs the risk of collateral damage to civilian population. Moreover, the history of counter insurgency operations in different parts of the world, Syria, Iraq and Afghanistan being the latest example, have demonstrated that such strikes have never weakened the capability of insurgent groups.

Conclusion

Responses have been confined to being reactive on most of the occasions. It is not surprising, therefore, that the least provocative action the government has taken, in the wake of major terrorist strike in the past is to suspend or cancel talks. Indian experience has shown that cancellation or suspension of talks have not yielded any positive results. Another disadvantage of cancellation or suspension of talks has been that the absence of talks has strengthened hardliners in both the countries. Lack of effective communication during suspension of talks has given room for further suspicion and trust deficit.

Negotiations have the potential to arrest further escalation of mistrust and resultant crisis. It helps both the sides in maintaining status quo and gives room to moderate elements to strengthen peace constituency by helping in creation of a conducive environment.

However, high expectation and media glare during every round of talks have proved to be counterproductive, particularly in situations where people from both the countries expect immediate tangible outcomes. It is in India's interest to engage Pakistan in talks by de-linking it with terror without much tangible realistic expectations. We must also acknowledge the fact that such talks are protracted in nature, help create conducive environment and reduce trust deficit. Therefore, the dialogue process must take into account possibilities of disruption and in that context, the Pathankot attacks should not have come as a surprise. In the past, such re-engagement even as Pakistan exports terror, encourages it to persist with its rougish conduct. It would be premature at this juncture to expect that Pakistan will take any concrete step to dismantle terrorist infrastructure on its soil.

On the Indian side, available information on responses since May 2014 has not suggested any concrete, coherent strategic roadmap to provide sufficient incentives to Pakistan to re-assess its current approach towards India. Therefore, even if installation of new government and its public pronouncements may appear to have elevated India's resolve of tough action against Pakistan in case of a terrorist attack; it has not increased India's capacity to coerce its neighbours into specific outcome.

Endnotes

1. "Ek Bharat, Shreshtha Bharat: SabkaSaath, SabkaVikas", BJP Election Manifesto 2014, accessed at: http://www.bjp.org/images/pdf_2014/full_manifesto_english_07 04.2014.pdf.
2. Resolution on Foreign Policy passed in BJP National Executive Meeting at Bengaluru (Karnataka), Friday, April 3, 2015, accessed at:

http://www.bjp.org/en/media-resources/press-releases/resolution-on-foreign-policy-passed-in-bjp-national-executive-meeting-at-bengaluru-karnataka.

3. R. Jagannathan, "Modifesto Points to Foreign Policy Shifts: No Primacy to US", accessed at: http://www.firstpost.com/world/modifesto-points-to-foreign-policy-shifts-no-primacy-to-us-1472799.html.
4. Ankit Panda, "Foreign Policy in 2014 BJP Manifesto", accessed at: http://thediplomat.com /2014/04/ foreign- policy -in- the-2014-bjp-manifesto.
5. "Nawaz Sharif to Attend Modi's Swearing-in Xeremony", *The Hindu*, New Delhi, May 24, 2014.
6. *The Hindu*, New Delhi, August 19, 2015.
7. In 2014, more than 550 incidents of ceasefire violation were reported along Jammu and Kashmir's Line of Control (LoC) and International Border (IB), with increased shelling, firing, Border Action Team (BAT) and sniper attacks, the highest since the truce came into force in 2003. In 2013, there were 347 ceasefire violations by Pakistan.
8. Salman Haider, "From Ufa to Square One", *Indian Express*, New Delhi, August 25, 2015.
9. The JeM is a terrorist group based in Pakistan. The group was formed on January 31, 2000, by Maulana Masood Azhar in Karachi after he was released from an Indian jail during the terrorist hostage swap of December 31, 1999, following the hijacking of an IC-814, an Indian Airlines flight from Kathmandu to Delhi. The outfit has been banned by the Indian government under provisions of the Prevention of Terrorism Act (POTA) on October 25, 2001. The US Department of State has also designated the outfit as a foreign terrorist organisation. The JeM received training and weapons from the ISI and worked closely with Al-Qaeda. It has been held responsible for the December 13, 2001 terrorist attack on the Indian Parliament in New Delhi. The outfit was involved in a number of terrorist attacks in India, including attack on Indian Parliament in December 2001. Though the group is technically banned in Pakistan, it enjoys the continuing patronage of the ISI.
10. On July 27, 2015 three terrorists in army uniform attacked the Dina Nagar police station in Gurdaspur district of Punjab. The

attack resulted in the death of three civilians and four policemen, including a superintendent of police; fifteen others were injured. All three attackers were killed in the operation, which lasted almost 12 hours. In addition, five bombs were found on the Amritsar-Pathankot line on a rail-bridge near Parmanand railway station. Also see, Vikram Sood, "Pathankot Attack: Someone is Unhappy with Modi-Nawaz Talks", accessed at: http://www.rediff.com/news/column/pathankot-attack-someone-is-unhappy-with-modi-nawaz-talks/20160103.htm.

11. Shruti Singh, "Pathankot Terror Attack Planned by ISI: The Inside Story", accessed at: http://indiatoday.intoday.in/story/pathankot-terror-attack-planned-by-isi-the-inside-story/1/560715.html.
12. "Pathankot to Mazar, Terror Trail Leads Sleuths to ISI's Footprints", accessed at: http://www.newindianexpress .com /nation/Pathankot-to-Mazar-Terror-Trail-Leads-Sleuths-to-ISIs-Footprints/2016/01/07/article3215641.ece.
13. "Pathankot Attack Aimed at Probing Modi Govt's Red Lines", C. Christine Fair, accessed at: http://www.business-standard.com/article/current-affairs/pathankot-attack-aimed-at-probing-modi-govt-s-red-lines-c-christine-fair-116010900252_1.html.
14. "Pak ISI Responsible For Pathankot Attack: Bruce Riedel", accessed at: http://www.newindianexpress.com/nation/Pak-ISI-Responsible-For-Pathankot-Attack-Bruce-Riedel/2016/01/06/article3214343.ece.
15. Bruce Riedel, "Blame Pakistani Spy Service for Attack on Indian Air Force Base", accessed at: http://www.thedailybeast.com/articles/2016/01/05/blame-pakistani-spy-service-for-attack-on-indian-air-force-base.html.
16. Vikram Sood, "Pathankot Attack: Someone is Unhappy with Modi-Nawaz Talks", accessed at: http://www.rediff.com/news/column/pathankot-attack-someone-is-unhappy-with-modi-nawaz-talks/20160103.htm.
17. Frederic Grare, "India-Pakistan Relations: Does Modi Matter?", *The Washington Quarterly*, 37:4, Winter 2015, pp. 101-115.
18. Ibid.
19. Ishaan Tharoor, "The Pakistani Origins of the Israeli State", *The*

Washington Post, December 3, 2014, accessed at: https://www.washingtonpost.com/news/worldviews/wp/2014/12/03/the-pakistani-origins-of-the-israeli-state. Also see, Faisal Devji, "Muslim Zion: Pakistan as a Political Idea", Harvard University Press, 2013.

20. For a detailed discussion on the subject, see, Faisal Devji, "Muslim Zion: Pakistan as a Political Idea", Harvard University Press, 2013.
21. Ibid, p. 47.
22. Sumit Ganguly, "Conflict Unending: India-Pakistan Tensions Since 1947", New York, Columbia University Press, 2001.
23. C. Christine Fair, "Fighting to the End: The Pakistan Army's Way of War", Oxford University Press, 2014.
24. S.K. Datta, "Inside ISI: The Story and Involvement of the ISI in Afghan Jihad, Taliban, Al-Qaeda, 9/11, Osama Bin Laden, 26/11 and the Future of Al-Qaeda", New Delhi, Vij Books, 2014.
25. Frederic Grare, "After Modi's Big Win: Can India and Pakistan Enhance Relations?", accessed at: http://carnegieendowment.org/2014/08/11/after-modi-s-big-win-can-india-and-pakistan-enhance-relations.
26. S. Kalyanraman, "Operation Parakram: An Indian Exercise in Coercive Diplomacy", *Strategic Analysis*, Vol. 26, Issue 4, 2002, pp. 478-492.
27. Ibid.
28. "Post-26/11, India Considered Surgical Air Strikes: Ex-Pak Foreign Minister Kasuri", accessed at: http://www.firstpost.com/india/post-2611-india-considered-surgical-air-strikes-ex-pak-foreign-minister-kasuri-2456546.html.
29. "India Can't Afford to Carry Out Surgical Strikes Inside Pakistan", Sartaj Aziz says, accessed at: http://timesofindia.indiatimes.com/india/India-cant-afford-to-carry-out-surgical-strikes-inside-Pakistan-Sartaj-Aziz-says/articleshow/44838758.cms.
30. Lalit Mansingh, "Should India Carry Out Surgical Strikes in Pak?", accessed at: http://www.outlookindia.com/magazine/story/should-india-carry-out-surgical-strikes-in-pak/239502.

4

India's Policy towards Indian Communities Living Abroad

V. Suryanarayan

India is weak today and cannot do much for her children abroad. But she does not forget them and every insult to them is humiliation and sorrow for her. A day will come when her long arm will protect them and her strength will compel justice to them—*Jawaharlal Nehru, Message to the Indian National Congress, 1939.*

What we seek is a broader relationship, in fact, a partnership among all children of Mother India, so that our country can emerge as a major global player. We value the role of people of Indian origin as unofficial ambassadors providing a link between India and the rest of the world—*Atal Behari Vajpayee, former Prime Minister of India.*

To be an Indian outside India has several complex facets. The commonly used term for these people is Diaspora. The Singhvi Committee Report uses this term. The term Diaspora is Jewish in origin and does not exactly convey the complexities of these communities. It was used to refer to Jewish communities "living in exile outside Palestine" consequent to the seizure of their homeland by foreign powers. The Jews were subjected to severe persecution and they fanned out to different parts of the world. However, throughout centuries, they hankered for their homeland. There was a special relationship between the land of Israel and the Jewish people.

However, if we analyse the spread of Indian communities

abroad, there were several "pull and push" factors. And what is more, most of them will not return to India. Equally unsatisfactory is the term "Indians Overseas" popularized by political sociologists. A vast majority belongs to the third or fourth generation and has become a permanent feature of the demographic profile of the countries in which they have settled. They would like to be referred to as Malaysians or Singaporeans or South Africans of Indian origin, rather than a Overseas Indians. The people of Indian origin are, slowly, but surely, becoming distinct communities, with certain cultural affinities with the land of their forefathers, but also different in many respects from these societies. Cultural persistence—retaining many aspects of their culture in an alien environment and adaptation to new surroundings—are twin facets of these dynamic groups.

The second generation ABCDs—American Born Confused Desis—do not have a coherent answer to the question: where are you from? The clash of cultures and values results in loyalty to both India and America. The first generation teaches the second, values about the motherland. But to them values get a little bit complicated—Indian at home and American in the public place. On their visits to India their American accented English is a source of endless amusement to the relatives.

The second largest Diaspora in the world, next only to the Chinese, the people of Indian origin are scattered across the world. When the Encyclopaedia of Indian Diaspora was published in 2006, there were only five countries in the world, which did not have an Indian element in its population. The five were: Mauritania, North Korea, Romania, Guinea Bissau and Cape Verde islands. All the other countries have a sprinkling of Indian community, complete with Hindu temples, Moslem mosques and Christian churches, curry shops selling tandoori chicken and idli and dosa with filter coffee and celebration of festivals like Deepavali and Holi.

The Singhvi Committee Report estimates their number to

be about 20 million, which is an under estimate. According to informed sources, their number should be around 35 million. What is more, there is also the Diaspora of the Diaspora. The descendants of the Indians who went to the Caribbean, for example, have migrated to United States, Australia and Canada. Diaspora, therefore, is like the scattering of the seed in the wind, the fruits of which are a new creation. Understanding Diaspora is like self-realization and self-recognition. Prof. Bikhu Parekh has summed it up beautifully: "The Diasporic Indian is like the banyan tree, the national symbol of the Indian way of life, he spreads out his roots in several soils, drawing nourishment from one when the rest dries up. Far from being homeless, he has several homes, and that is the only way he increasingly comes to feel at home in the world".

Sometimes the diasporic Indian loses his identity. Take the case of two Malaysian leaders Dr. Mahathir, the former Prime Minister and Anwar Ibrahim, former Deputy Prime Minister. Mahathir's father was a Moslem from Malabar, but Mahathir identifies himself as a Malay and rarely speaks about his Indian ancestry. Similarly, Anwar's ancestors were Moslems from Tamil Nadu, but he has also completely identified himself with Malay way of life.

The term Diaspora is generally used as an all encompassing term to cover all categories of Indians who live abroad. From an academic point of view, the distinction in terms of their legal status should be highlighted:

1. People of Indian origin who have become citizens of the countries in which they have settled.
2. All those Indians who have neither taken Indian citizenship nor the citizenship of the countries in which they have settled. These are the "stateless people". The legal status of the "stateless people" was a thorny issue which vitiated India's relations with Sri Lanka for several years after Independence. Though the problem in most countries has been satisfactorily resolved, it still remains to

be sorted out in few countries.

According to the Singhvi Committee Report, the people of Indian origin in Myanmar number 2.9 million, of which 400,000 are stateless persons. In Malaysia, according to Singhvi Committee Report, there are 50,000 stateless Indians. The HINDRAF maintains that their number is around 100,000. Unfortunately, the problems faced by the stateless people do not figure in the deliberations of the Pravasi Bharatiya Divas. New Delhi should take up this matter with the host governments on a priority basis and resolve the issue amicably.

3. Indian citizens who have gone abroad for specific purposes. Majority of Indians working in West Asian countries belong to this category.
4. Overseas Citizenship of India. This scheme came into force in 2006 as a response to the persistent demands of the Indian community living in Western countries for dual citizenship. People of Indian origin, who have taken citizenship of various countries, can apply for Overseas Citizenship of India. Their application will be considered on an individual basis and after careful scrutiny they will be granted Overseas Citizenship of India. They will enjoy all the rights of Indian citizens, except the right to vote and the right to stand for election. In other words, Overseas Indian citizenship should not be confused with dual citizenship. Exact number of those who have been conferred Overseas Indian citizenship is not known, but according to the Ministry of Overseas Indian Affairs, as on May 31, 2013, 12.25 lakh of OCI registration booklets were issued.

The Indian communities abroad are not a homogenous group. They are divided on the basis of their religion—Hinduism, Christianity, Islam and Sikhism and on the basis of language—Tamil, Malayalam, Hindi, Telugu etc. In Malaysia and Singapore, the term Indian encompasses Indians, Pakistanis, Bangladeshis, Nepalese and Sri Lankans. Fiji provides an interesting exception. Regardless of which part of India they come from—Andhra Pradesh, Uttar Pradesh, Bihar, Kerala or Tamil Nadu—they created a new community, where everybody spoke Fijian Hindi. In this beautiful land, multiplicity of cultures did not clash, but as a result of constant interaction and inter-marriage, a new society and a new language evolved. One of the interesting and creative books in Fijian Hindi is written by Professor Subramani. It is a special kind of Hindi, which is not spoken in India. Subramani, whose ancestors came from Tamil Nadu, also speaks and writes in Fijian Hindi. *Dauka Puran* is the only book of its kind, the first and only substantial literary text, produced in that language. It has appeared at a time, when the educated Fijian leaders, as a result of political discrimination, are migrating in large numbers to United States, Canada and Australia. Perhaps, Fijians of a later generation may not speak this language; they may speak English, or they may speak standard Hindi. And that will be a great tragedy!

The Diaspora defies easy categorization. Due to their varied origins, different patterns of migration and differing degrees of integration, simple generalizations can lead us nowhere. Therefore, it would be simplistic and naïve to assume that the problems that these people face and what the future holds for them are identical. Their problems are intertwined with the nature of their migration, their social and economic status, the size of the community, educational attainments and the majority-minority syndrome in the countries in which they have settled.

In some countries like South Africa and Southern Rhodesia, they were until very recently subjected to varying forms of discrimination, in Mauritius, Guyana, Malaysia, Singapore, Sri Lanka and Trinidad, they share political power; in Fiji, though they were the majority community, they have been effectively deprived of political power; in United States, they are one of the most affluent groups, an object of envy and admiration; and nearer home in Sri Lanka, the people of Indian origin were converted into a merchandise to be divided between the two countries in the name of good neighbourly relations.

Cycles of Migration

The movement of Indians abroad, in historical and cultural perspective, can be divided into three sequential parts. The first phase, which began with the first century AD with the migration of Indian merchants, princes and artisans led to the cultural efflorescence of Southeast Asian countries. Angkor Wat, Lara Djonggrang and Borobudur stand testimony to the benign cultural interaction between India and the Southeast Asian peoples. Indian historians, during the nationalist movement, with pardonable exaggeration, referred to the transmission of Indian cultural forms as the making of "Greater India".

With the development of maritime trade and founding of maritime empires in the oceanic world, Indian traders from east and west coasts of India began to settle down in the coastal areas. They inter-married with the local people and got culturally assimilated with them. To illustrate, Gujarati and Chulia merchants began to trade with Southeast Asia, exchanging Indian made textiles with Southeast Asian spices. Mention should be made about Malacca Chetties, a miniscule community, who got converted to Islam, but retained some of the Indian cultural forms like the worship of God Ganesha.

If one leaves aside this glorious chapter in the history of India, the contacts with the outside world, especially during the colonial period, had been accompanied by sorrow, misery and impoverishment. Imperialist domination made India the pivot of the British Empire and the vast reservoir of manpower was exploited to serve the colonial interests of Great Britain. Large army of labourers, soldiers, convicts, clerks and money lenders settled in different parts of the Empire to serve the politico-economic interests of Britain.

Lord Curzon, the British Viceroy, explained India's contribution to the expansion of the British Empire as follows:

"If you want to save your colony of Natal from being overrun by a formidable enemy, you ask India for help and she gives it; if you want to rescue White Men's legations from massacres at Peking, and the need is urgent, you request the Government of India to dispatch an expedition and they dispatch it; if you are fighting the Mad Mullah in Somaliland, you can soon discover that Indian troops and Indian General are best qualified for the task and you ask the Government of India to send them; if you want to defend any of your extreme outposts or coaling stations of the Empire, Aden, Mauritius, Singapore, Hong Kong, even Tien-Tsin, it is to the Indian army you turn; if you want to build a railway to Uganda or in the Sudan, you apply for Indian labour...It is with Indian coolie labour that you exploit the plantations equally of Demerara and Natal; with Indian trained officers you irrigate the dam in the Nile; with Indian forest officers that you tap the resources of Central Africa and Siam, with Indian surveyors that you explore all the hidden places of the earth".

Curzon's candid and forthright statement enables us to understand some of the factors that led to the movement of Indian labourers to different parts of the British Empire. The "coolies" who constituted the majority of the labourers were subjected to pull and push factors. The grinding poverty at home, worsened by regular famines, pushed them across the seas and the hope of eking out a decent living acted as a powerful "pull" factor. Prof. Hugh Tinker, the British historian, refers to this phenomenon as a "new form of slavery". The recruits were mainly from the Tamil areas of Madras Presidency and from the United Provinces and Bihar in northern India. The journey to Calcutta port was long and arduous. The life in the depots in Kolkata, where the labourers stayed before getting into the ship was another source of misery. It was dirty and filthy; what is more, the workers did not get sufficient food. The passage to the colonies was harrowing.

According to a background note prepared by the India

Office in London, the voyage of the "Mercahantman" which set sail to British Guyana had 385 Indian labourers of which 375 reported sick and 120 of them dying on the way. Those who complained of lack of medical facilities were disciplined with the use "rattan". As far as Tamil labourers who went to Ceylon, most of them were in a state of chronic indebtedness. They were lured by the Kanganies who advanced them some money to meet the expenses relating to sea travel and starting the life anew in alien surroundings. These workers also suffered innumerable hardships on their way to tea plantations. They suffered from fever and dysentery and when they fell ill they were driven off or allowed to die. The indebtedness to the Kanganies trapped them in a vicious system of slavery.

Charlie (CF) Andrews, the great friend of Mahatma Gandhi, whom the Indians Overseas affectionately called as the *deenabandhu* (friend of the downtrodden) told Gandhiji in South Africa that the issue in hand was a question of India's honour and that there could be no sacrifice of honour. Learning about the atrocious conditions in which the indentured labourers worked in Fiji, Andrews undertook the long journey to that place. He was appalled by the "filthy" lines, where men and women were herded like cattle with no respect for sanctity of human life. For several years, Andrews carried on a relentless struggle to put an end to the indenture system.

What about the planters? They were the favoured lot of the British government. They were given subsidies and incentives, including tax benefits; land was made available at cheap rates and railways were constructed to link the plantations to the Colombo port.

The agony and suffering undergone by the Indian coolies under the Planters Raj and the British Raj are innumerable. The verdant carpet of green in the central parts of Sri Lanka, which has made the country the veritable "island paradise" was due to the sweat and agony of the plantation workers. I would like to give two vignettes of the contrasting lives of the planters and the workers. While teaching in the Peradeniya University few years ago, I came across the Memoirs of Philip Crowe, US Ambassador to Ceylon in the 1950's, entitled *Diversions of a Diplomat in Ceylon.*

To quote Philip Crowe: "The estate bungalows are roomy, surrounded by lovely gardens. Servants are plentiful and relatively cheap. Social life is mainly limited to the local club consisting of a tennis court and a bar. There at weekends the planters gather for bridge, gossip, drink, billiards and tennis. Somerset Maugham might not find the makings of a great novel immediately, but the pleasures of life in the small tea communities are apparent". C.V. Velu Pillai, the sensitive Indian Tamil poet and political activist, has described the workers' lives as follows: "Here is but a row of tin roofed lines, the very warehouse where selfdom thrives; with a scant space of ten by twelve, there is the hearth, home drenched in soot and smoke, to eat and sleep, to incubate and breed, to meet the master's need".

The Mauritian poet Visvamitra Ganga Aashutosh has described how the Indian workers transformed, despite heavy odds, the economy of British colonies. To quote: "No gold did they find, underneath any stone they touched and turned, yet, every stone they touched into solid gold they turned".

The odyssey of Indian workers to different corners of the world had been a saga of courage and adventure. It is a tribute to their patience and forbearance in the face of hardship, rebuke and persecution that they produced some of the great leaders of these countries. The Making of the Mahatma, to quote Prof. Chandran Devenesan's phrase, took place in South Africa and his struggle against racial discrimination inspired a whole generation of nationalists in different parts of the world. Out of those freedom movements emerged great leaders like Dr. Cheddy Jagan of British Guyana, Seeweesagar Rangoolam of Mauritius, Yusuf Dadoo and Monty Naicker of South Africa, Savumyamurthy Thondaman of Sri Lanka, Devan Nair of Singapore, Jegannath Lechuman of Surinam, Sambandan of

Malaysia and many others. Through dint of hard work and education, children and grand children of these indentured labourers made a niche for themselves in their chosen professions. They include Nobel Laureate V.S. Naipaul, Sridath Ramphal, Aneerood Jegannauth, Sivanaraine Chandra Pal, Muthiah Muralitharan and many others. As former Prime Minister Vajpayee put it: "Few people who entered foreign lands can claim such testimony".

The post-Independence era witnessed another pattern of Indian migration. The economic expansion of Britain, coupled with the establishment of a welfare state, opened up opportunities for many qualified Indians in services, industry and professions. The technological breakthrough in the United States and Washington's policy of attracting the best talents led to an exodus of highly qualified and educated people to the United States. Similarly, the economic boom in West Asia since the 1970's led to the migration of large number of Indians to the countries of this region. These countries lacked manpower and skills and since India was willing to supply both at competitive rates, many countries turned to India to meet a variety of needs.

The world outside attracted some of the best Indian talents and brains and given the competitive nature of the Western world, the Indians became more innovative and dynamic abroad than while they were in India. Few names deserve special mention. They include Nobel Laureates Amartya Sen, Dr. Chandrasekhar and Dr. Ramakrishnan; economist Jagadish Bhagwati, ECG Sundarsen, Hargobind Khurana, Zubin Mehta, Kalpana Chawla and Fareed Zachariah. They have contributed to change the image of India from a country of hewers of wood and drawers of water to a nation on the march, throbbing with ideas, indomitable energy and zest for glory.

In a world of shrinking geographical boundaries and widening intellectual horizon, the Diaspora is getting closely knit among themselves and with their motherland. The Bharatiya Janata Party (BJP) had strong links with sections of the Diaspora in the Western World and, therefore, it was but natural that when it came to power it should strive to bring about closer links between India and the Diaspora. What is more, the phenomenal contribution of Overseas Chinese to the economic transformation of China made the Indian policy makers formulate new policies to establish economic links between the two.

The symbolic launching of this policy took place on January 9, 2003 when the Pravasi Bharatiya Divas was celebrated on a grand scale. On January 9, 1915 Mahatma Gandhi returned from South Africa and that day was chosen to provide historical links with the past. It should also be pointed out that the film industry, represented by Bollywood, Kollywood and Mollywood played a catalytic role in globalizing Indian culture and connecting the sub-continent with the Diaspora. The Diasporic literature, especially the writings of V.S. Naipaul, Salman Rushdie, Robinton Mistry, Amitav Ghosh and Vikram Seth portrayed vividly the lives of the Diasporic Indians and contributed to sensitizing the Indian people about the children of Mother India settled abroad.

Nationalist Response

To what extent have these policies succeeded? In order to make a proper evaluation, it is necessary to keep in mind the twists and turns of Indian polices towards Indian Diaspora in a historical perspective. A comparison with Overseas Chinese has important lessons for us. Historically, the Chinese and the Indians Overseas had always been subjected to pulls and pressures from their motherland. In the beginning, it was mainly economic, and large sums of money flowed to India and China. But with the growth of nationalism, political pulls also started exerting in a subtle way.

Just as Mahatma Gandhi's baptism in politics took place in South Africa in defence of the Indian community, the initial activities of the revolutionary government in China were related to Chinese communities abroad. Dr. Sun Yat Sen himself was a migrant from Honolulu, who had his higher education in Hong Kong. The Nationalist Government after the Revolution in 1911, started a Ministry of Overseas Chinese. Consulates were opened in Malaya, East Indies and Hong Kong. What is more, the new Government enunciated a new principle of citizenship. The doctrine of "once a Chinese always a Chinese" was proclaimed. It meant that citizenship went by ethnic origin and not by the place of birth. It had dangerous implications and was viewed with suspicion by the colonial governments and Southeast Asian nationalists.

The Indian nationalists, especially Mahatma Gandhi and Jawaharlal Nehru, were far more sensitive to the cross currents of international politics and the xenophobic tendencies of the nationalist leaders of many Asian countries, where the Indian communities were settled. While expressing concern for their abject living conditions, Gandhi and Nehru, at the same time, exhorted the Indians to live amicably with the local people. For example, in November 1927, at the end of a visit to Ceylon, Gandhiji told the Reddiar Sangham in Colombo: "I would leave one or two thoughts with you before I leave Colombo. Since you are earning your bread in this beautiful land, I would ask you to live as sugar in milk. Even as a cup of milk which is full to the brim does not overflow when sugar is gently added to it, the sugar accommodating itself in the milk and enriching its taste, in the same way, I would like you to live in the island so as not to become interlopers and so as to enrich the lives of the people in whose midst you are living".

The Indian nationalist leaders were also sensitive to the fact that sections of the Indian population were exploiting the local people. The usurious money lending practices of the Nattukottai Chettiars in Burma led to a situation where one third of the arable land in lower Burma came under the possession of absentee Indian Chettiars. The Indian working class in Rangoon was despised by the Burmese because of their addiction to liquor and overcrowding in the slums. The position was aggravated when few Indian Muslims resorted to marrying Burmese women and leaving them in the lurch when they returned to India. The cumulative effect was large scale anti-Indian riots in Burma in 1937.

During his visit to Ceylon in 1939, Jawaharlal Nehru became conscious of the anti-Indian character of Sinhalese leaders. In fact, in the Asian Relations Conference held in New Delhi in March-April 1947, there were under-currents of protest against the exploitative nature of the rich Indians living in neighbouring countries. Despite these anti-India sentiments, Nehru believed that once India became independent, it would adopt a dynamic policy towards Indians Overseas which would enhance their prestige among the local people and confer them dignity. The quotation from Jawaharlal Nehru's message, quoted in the beginning of this essay, bears ample testimony to this fact.

Post-Independence Phase

The hope that independent India would pursue a realistic policy after Independence was soon belied. Colombo enacted citizenship legislations which excluded large sections of local Indian population from citizenship. The problem of stateless people continued without an end until 1964, when the Sirimavo-Shastri pact was signed. In a reversal of well-known principles laid down by Jawaharlal Nehru, New Delhi decided to take back large number of people of Indian origin as Indian citizens. Colombo took shelter under the argument that it was a sovereign country and it had the right to prescribe qualifications for conferring citizenship. In the same way, India was a pathetic spectator when large number of Tamils living in Burma were edged out as a result of socialistic policies pursued by the Burmese government. In a speech in the Parliament, Nehru admitted: "I entirely agree with any criticism that may be made that we have not been able to do anything substantial in regard to the Indians in Commonwealth". The cumulative effect was New Delhi pursuing a policy of non-involvement with the Overseas

Indians, except making occasional pious statements that New Delhi's policy was to encourage Indians Overseas to integrate with the local population.

A major change in India's policy took place when Rajiv Gandhi became the Prime Minister. The change was occasioned by the developments in Fiji, when the popularly elected government, which had a fair sprinkling of Indian members, was overthrown in a military coup led by Sitiveni Rabuka on May 14, 1987. A period of wanton disregard of human rights followed. Number of Indo-Fijian leaders was subjected to violence and humiliation. The economy began to collapse. In a rare act of statesmanship, Rajiv Gandhi mobilized international opinion against Rabuka and saw to it that Fiji was expelled from the Commonwealth.

While it was definitely a feather in the cap of New Delhi, it must be pointed out that Indo-Fijians are still searching for security, dignity and identity. As Prof. Brij V. Lal has pointed out, "After more than a century, Indo-Fijians still struggle for political equality in the land of their birth. The deeply felt, but often unacknowledged need of the human soul to belong, to have a place of one's own, to be rooted, is denied to them. How long, they ask, should a people live in a place before they are allowed to call it home"?

Role of Indian Diaspora in Economic Transformation

Since Narendra Modi assumed power as Prime Minister, a more concerted and vigorous policy is being pursued towards Indians Overseas. New Delhi has started viewing them not as a liability, but as an asset. It is hoped that the Diaspora will become an invaluable component of India's foreign policy, in much the same way as the Jewish Diaspora in the United States influences their foreign policy. Narendra Modi, in his frequent foreign visits, makes it a point to address the Indian communities; this gesture has elicited magnificent response in the United States, United Kingdom, Australia, Fiji, Malaysia and Singapore. Narendra Modi wants to turn every Indian abroad into an ambassador of India. He has repeatedly urged the community to contribute money, time and technical expertise to his programmes, including the cleaning up of the Ganga, making India garbage free and constructing rural toilets. He called upon the Indians abroad to visit India regularly and give a fillip to tourism.

It may be pointed out that the Overseas Chinese has contributed immensely to the economic transformation of China. If China can tap the resources and entrepreneurial skills of the Overseas Chinese, why should India lag behind? In 1976, when the Singapore statesman Lee Kuan Yew visited China, he told the Chinese leaders, "We Singapore Chinese are the descendants of landless peasants from Guangdong and Fujian in South China, whereas the scholars, Mandarins and literati had stayed and left their progeny in China. There was nothing that Singapore had done which China could not do, and do better". Lee Kuan Yew and Dr. Goh Keng Swee provided valuable advice which led to the establishment of export promotion zones (EPZs). The EPZs and the industrial parks gave a boost to China's industrialization and modernization. Today, China has become the factory of the world.

While analyzing the relevance of the Chinese model to India, it must be highlighted that Indians who live abroad are not *Kamadehenus*. For example, the Indians constitute 8 percent of the population of Malaysia, but they own only 1.4 percent of the national wealth. In Singapore, the most developed country in our region, according to the informed sources, the per capita income of a Singapore citizen of Indian origin is less than the national average. Moreover, the earlier Indian experience was that the wealthy Indians would prefer to keep their savings in Swiss banks rather than invest in India. Well-known columnist, K. Subramanyam has pointed out that New Delhi came to know to its dismay that the wealthy Indians who were expelled by Idi Amin from Uganda had all their wealth deposited in Swiss banks. None of them returned to India, they settled down in England and started their lives anew. I.G. Patel, former economic advisor to the Government of India, mentioned, in the course of the Lal Bahadur Shastri Memorial lecture few years ago, "the Overseas Indian may have his heart in India but he would prefer to keep his money in the Swiss banks".

Can Prime Minister Narendra Modi and his government bring about a fundamental transformation in the economic outlook of the wealthy Indians who have settled abroad? Certain economic indicators are worth mentioning. India is the world's leading receiver of financial remittances, claiming more than 12 percent of the world's remittances in 2007. In 2014, remittances to India stood at US$ 70.39 billion, accounting for 4 percent of India's GDP. NRI deposits are also huge. In 2014, NRI deposits were estimated to be US$ 121.8 billion. During President Obama's visit to India in January 2015, it was announced that a new public-private partnership will be started to enable Indian Diaspora to invest in India.

Indian Diaspora can act as a catalyst in the "Make in India" programme through remittances, foreign direct investment, transfer of knowledge and entrepreneurial networks. Since the Indian community dominates information technology and IT-enabled services in developed countries, they can play a positive role in India's technological revolution.

As pointed out earlier, compared to China, the Diasporic involvement in India had been modest. The formation of the Overseas Indian Facilitation Centre (OIFC) to further investment and entrepreneurial ties between the Indian Diaspora and their homeland is a positive step in the right direction. It is the level of business comfort and profitability of business operations which will attract FDI into India.

As an academic, I would plead for the effective utilization of Indian academics, scientists, doctors and engineers settled abroad for starting joint ventures in the field of higher education. The Ministry of External Affairs, which has been strengthened recently with the incorporation of the Ministry of

Overseas Indian Affairs, should in right earnest bring about the necessary changes in the productive environment in the country, especially the provision of infrastructure and reduction of transaction costs. Will the private-public partnership rise to the occasion? Only time can provide the answer.

5

Faultlines in India's Neighbourhood Policy and Nepal's Quest for Identity

Pavitran K.S.

India and Nepal have age old relations. Despite the asymmetry in size, the two countries and people have nurtured unshakable links since the time of Gautham Budha. [1] However, the contemporary nation state of Nepal is of relatively recent origin, dating back only to the last decades of the eighteenth century. The geo-strategic position of Nepal has attracted the attention of not only India and China but all the major powers as well. Nepal has an area of 1,47,181 square kilometres and a population of more than 27 million. [2] It is surrounded by India on three sides and shares a border of over 1,850 kilometres to the south with five Indian states—Bihar, Sikkim, West Bengal, Uttar Pradesh and Uttarakhand. British India regarded Nepal as a buffer between India and Russia. British government signed a treaty with Rana government of Nepal in 1923 recognising independence and sovereignty of Nepal thus maintaining good relations with Nepal. The independent India also considered it as a buffer which skirts five hundred miles of its northern border along the People's Republic of China and on the southern slopes of the Himalayas.

Nehruvian Beginnings

India and Nepal bear a complex nature of relationship, which is not oriented of political factors alone but covers the entire gamut of socio-cultural and economic issues. More than 7 million ethnic Nepalese live and work in India and the Indian Army has at least 46 Gurka battallions. During the time of Nehru, he wanted to create a security zone around India's neighbourhood where Cold War politics could be kept at bay. Thus on July 31, 1950, 'The Treaty of Peace and Friendship' and 'The Treaty of Commerce and Trade' were signed by India and Nepal. The Treaty of Peace and Friendship required India and Nepal to consult mutually on matters relating to national security. The Treaty recognised Nepal's sovereignty, territorial integrity and independence. Addressing the Lok Sabha in December 1950, Nehru stated that India permitted Nepal to "develop other foreign relations". [3]

The fact is that the Nepalese National Congress was formed in India in 1946 and depends on Indian national leadership for guidance and support. India being the dominant partner in this 'special relationship', exercises immense and decisive influence over the affairs of Nepal. India also wanted Nepal to take its strategic interests into account in following its own independent foreign policy. India played an important role in overthrowing the Rana rule and eventually in restoration of monarchy in Nepal and is keen to establish friendly relations with Nepal more for its own interest than for the Nepalese people. [4] Thus, despite being sympathetic to democratic forces, India had to support monarchy at times. From Indira Gandhi to Manmohan Singh, India followed the same established pattern of foreign policy shaped by Nehru. India realised that stability at times was more important than establishment of democracy.

After the accession to thrown in 1955, King Mahendra took up the task of defining the fundamentals of Nepal's foreign policy. He believed that Nepal's identity and self-image were possible only by reducing its dependence over India.

In 1960, he dismissed the Koirala [5] government and captured the power. This led to the deterioration of relations with India. Anti-Indian sentiments and furtherance of Nepalese nationalism were major happenings which affected heavily the future course of actions at political level between the two countries. During the time of King Birendra, Nepal was declared as a "zone of peace". By 1955, as the process of change in the domestic and external milieu advanced in Nepal, the pattern of its 'special relations' with India also changed alternatively. Nepal started evolving the policy of balance of power in relation to the neighbouring region. The Panchsheel agreement between India and China prompted Nepal to normalise its relations with China.

The Sino-Indian conflict of October-November 1962 had the most salutary effect on both India and Nepal. Nepal maintained neutrality in the Sino-Indian conflict. However, Indo-Nepalese border trade was resumed. India started entering into a new relationship with Nepal based on the understanding that it was for Nepal to decide for itself the type of government that it should have and that Indian territory was not allowed to lean towards China. After the war of Bangladesh in 1971, India emerged as a pre-eminent power in South Asia. At this point, India's security concern, economic interdependence and Nepal's realisation of its limited manoeuvrability were some of the basic points of convergence of mutual national interests. [6]

India's foreign policy towards Nepal has three major and yet interrelated objectives—strategic political and economic. Strategic interest i.e. to meet any threat coming from China via Nepal....The political objective constituted mainly of maintaining a 'special relationship' under the 1950 treaty, countering the China and other powers., containment of communism, supporting a regime with a pro-Indian orientation, and looking after the interests of Nepalis of Indian origin and people of India living in Nepal. Its economic objective has been guided by two main considerations, to exert influence on harmonising economic policies between the two countries, and sharing water recourses for 'mutual benefits'. [7] The official establishment in India thinks that China's presence behind Nepal with the former's military consolidation in Tibet will naturally make Indo-Nepalese border much harder even as compared to Indo-Bangladesh and Indo-Burmese border. [8] Another reason is that the Nepali Maoists have linkages with Indian Maoists. The creation of a Compact Revolutionary Zone (CRZ) by the Nepal Maoists and Indian Maoists which extends from Nepal and stretch across more than five Indian states "hold certain advantages to the insurgents and thus have significant security implications for India". [9]

Economically, India has its own interests. Nepal is one of its large and most lucrative markets. Thus, a new trade treaty came into force on December 5, 1996, which set the ground rules for growth in trade and investment for future. On 22nd August 2009, with the visit of Madhav Kumar Nepal, Prime Minister of Nepal, India and Nepal initialled the revised Treaty of Trade and agreement of cooperation to control unauthorised trade [10] which will contribute to further enhancing bilateral trade.

At present, nearly all the Nepal's fuel imports come from the Indian Oil Corporation. The Nepalese rupee continues to be pegged to the Indian rupee. India is Nepal's main trading partner and the borders are open. Nepalis have served in the Indian Army, and receive pensions on retirement. One seventh of the entire population of Nepal resides and works in India. The overall quantum of India's assistance to Nepal is approximate ₹ 3,600 crore.

According to figures for the Nepalese fiscal year 2066 (July 2010), bilateral trade with India accounted for ₹ 16,129.7 crore which amounted to 58.7 percent of Nepal's total external trade. India and Nepal have a treaty of transit which confers transit rights theory in each others' territory through mutually agreed routes and modalities. The treaty was last renewed for seven years in March 2006. The two countries have concluded a Rail Services Agreement (RSA) and a revised Air Services Agreement (ASA) to enhance bilateral connectivity. India also remains Nepal's largest source of foreign investment and Indian investments in Nepal amounted to ₹ 1,586 crore with 462 FDI projects. India accounts for 44 percent of the total foreign investment in Nepal. Over the years, the framework of 1950 Treaty, which perhaps benefited India more than Nepal, has guided the Nepal-India relations basically at political and strategic level.

Political Developments in the New Millennium

It was Manmohan Adhikari, the former Nepal Prime Minister, who during a visit to India in 1995, officially requested for the first time to the Indian Government to revise the 1950 Treaty. However, the request was declined by India. India believes that the revision or termination of the Treaty will deny India the advantage of exercising unilateral option (implied though not stated under the Treaty) of meeting unforeseen security contingency in Nepal. As things stand today, though India has erected a creditable structure of defence along its border with China, abrogation of the Treaty would drastically undermine this deterrence. [11] Abrogation of the Treaty would also necessitate a drastic redefinition of the totality of Indo-Nepal relations.

The fact is that, Nepal's treaties and agreements with India were "conditioned more by short strategies of regime survival than by genuine national interests". [12] The passion of Nepalese ruling class to seek the support of Indian Government for their own survival and sustenance still continue. In short, the 1950 Treaty of Peace and Friendship created visible strains on the juridical claim of equal sovereignties with the Unified Communist Party of Nepal (Maoist)-UCPN (M) assuming power in 2008. Beginning with a 12 point understanding reached between the Seven Party Alliance (SPA) and the maoists in Delhi in November 2005, [13] the Government of India welcomed the roadmap laid down by the historic Comprehensive Peace Agreement of November 2006 towards political stabilisation and institutionalisation of multi-party democracy which culminated in the 2008 constituent assembly elections. However, the strain paved way to fissures as the Maoists in Nepal pledged to scrap the Treaty which guides the two countries 'special relationship'. [14]

During Prime Minister Prachanda's (Pushpa Kamal Dahal) visit to India in September 2008, both sides agreed to receive, adjust and update the 1950 Treaty of Peace and Friendship. However, India was not interested at that point of time, with the Maoists getting credit for giving Nepal a constitution and consolidating politically on that basis. It is in these circumstances that India helped to form a non-maoist government in Nepal.

In an interview on the circumstances leading to the dismissal of his country's army chief and his own subsequent resignation as Prime Minster, maoist leader Prachanda said that the maoists will prefer to sit in the opposition rather than see the authority of a democratically elected government undermined. [15] The army chief Gen. Katawal always remained firmly opposed to the democratisation of the army and did his best to scuttle the democratic process in Nepal. Matters came to a head when he disobeyed specific orders from the government on matters central to the implementation of Comprehensive Peace Agreement. India did little to get the Nepalese Army to back off, but sent clear signals to parties like the Communist Party of Nepal (United Marxist Leninist)-CPN (UML) and the Nepali Congress that they should oppose the maoists. [16]

The end result was that the Cabinet went ahead and exercised its prerogative to replace the army chief while the CPN (UML) walked out, thereby reducing Prachanda's government to a minority. At this stage, the President of Nepal, Ram Baran Yadav, overstepped his constitutional authority and "reinstated" the army chief. As a result, Prachanda resigned. The maoists say the issue at stake was not the fate of this particular army chief but the principle of civilian control. The constituent assembly that was elected in 2008 was dissolved in May 2012. The Mohan Baidya led maoists who split from the UCPN (M) in June 2012 alleged that with the trade agreement that the new Prime Minister, Baburam Bhattarai signed with the Indian Government in August 2011, the maoist leadership has compromised on Nepal's interests. [17]

The November 2013 elections for a new Constituent Assembly (CA-II) in Nepal gave a fractured mandate but one that made the traditional upper caste and upper class groups dominant again. [18] While the maoists have emerged as the single largest party in 2008 with 240 seats, the three Madhesis parties accounted for 84 seats—the outcome in 2013 elections turned out very differently. Maoists were down to 80 seats and the Madhesis parties which had splintered from three to a dozen, could only manage 40 seats. NC moved up from 115 seats in 2008 to 196 and the UML from 108 to 175 seats. In a way, the defeat of the maoists in the second constituent assembly elections was considered as an angry reaction of a highly frustrated electorate which had placed great hope in the maoists to lead the way in the realisation of a new progressive constitution, enduring peace, political stability and progressive socio-economic transformation. [19]

In the context of the new developments, the issue of updating the 1950 Treaty came up for discussion during the Joint Commission (JC) meeting held in Nepal on 26 July 2014. Prime Minister Narendra Modi's visit to Nepal in August 2014 was the first by an Indian Prime Minister after a gap of 17 years. In his speech at the Constituent Assembly, Modi spoke about respecting Nepali sovereignty and reiterated his readiness to revise the contentious 1950 Treaty in line with Nepali wishes and promised accelerated cooperation and generous terms for Nepal's power exports to India with US$ 250 million line of credit. The two governments signed a Power Trade Agreement (PTA) while GMR also concluded a Project Development Agreement (PDA) regarding a 900 MW hydel project on upper Karnali. Foreign secretary Jai Shanker's visit to Kathmandu in September 2015, has been a spur to Nepali nationalism which more often than not, carries strains of anti-Indianism.

New Constitution and Strains in Indo-Nepal Relations

On September 20, 2015, Nepal adopted its first democratic constitution. [20] President Ram Baran Yadav promulgated the charter. It creates seven states in a secular, federal system. The Constitution with 308 articles, 35 parts and 9 schedules was the culmination of seven years of effort including a failed first Constituent Assembly. This process began with the 12 point agreement of 2005, [21] negotiated between the underground maoists and Nepal's mainstream political parties, facilitated by New Delhi. [22] There are contradictions galore in the Constitution. However, the Constitution has progressive elements, like institutionalising the republic and secularism, confirming social and economic rights and rejecting the death penalty.

Moreover, amendments can be adopted with relative ease. Everything except sovereignty and national integrity are open to amendments. The new Constitution failed to satisfy the Madhesis, Tharus and Janjatis who together comprise 49 percent of the Nepal's population. They want two separate states having domination of the Madhesis and the Tharus. The state with a mix of plains and hills is not acceptable to them. Nepal has more than a hundred ethnic groups. However, it has always been ruled by Bahun-Chettri (Brahmin-Kshathriya) hill elite, which together with other hill upper castes, account for less than 30 percent of the population. The leadership of three major political parties—NC, CPN (UML) and UCPN (M)—belongs to this group. On the other hand, the Janjatis (hill tribes), Tharus (plains tribes), dalits and Madhesis have traditionally been the oppressed groups.

China has welcomed the new Constitution saying that as a "friendly neighbour", it hoped for increased stability and growth. India expressed displeasure about the new Constitution and asked Nepal to make as many as seven amendments to address the concerns of the Madhesis and the Janjatis. There are three major problems with the Constitution which prevents India from undermining the document. First, the federal-provincial demarcation is perceived to be unfair to the people of the Terai region; secondly, the constituency delimitation is skewed against the Madhes population as half the population, that is the Pahadi (hill) community gets 100 seats but the other half consisting of the Madhesi and Janjatis get only 65 seats. Finally, the 'proportional inclusion' clause, for reservation, includes many forward castes of the Pahadi region, which negates the principle of affirmative action.

Whatever may be the facts, there is a feeling in Nepal that India has overstepped the limits of suggestion and rather tried to impose its views onto a much smaller neighbour. New Delhi's support has been lopsided by focussing on the Madhes-based parties that have been demanding plains only provinces. If India's strategic interest forces a fait accompli of exclusively plains-based provinces, critiques points out that there are two possible outcomes. First, the massive weight of poverty of the plains will be locked in and the promise of federalism will likely be wasted. Second, this interference will create a politically unstable Nepal astride India's populous heartland. Thus, commentators on India-Nepal relations suggested a return to Panchsheel.

The relations between the two countries have strained since the Indian origin people living in southern parts of Nepal and Terai have protested violently against the new Constitution. The adoption of constitution in Nepal by overlooking the interests of the Indian origin Madhesis is seen as a single most diplomatic challenge for the Government of India. The Madhesis believe that the new constitution will lead to their marginalization in Nepal. India's support to the Madhes agitation against a discriminatory Constitution adopted in September 2015 had resulted in restricted supply of essential goods to Nepal for nearly six months, causing unprecedented hardship to Nepal's people and generating strong anti-India sentiments among the country's hill communities.

The blockade has alienated Nepal's political parties as well as the public opinion from India has exposed the Madhesi community to further vulnerability from Nepali national chauvinists who have always accused them of being a fifth column for India. Under these circumstances, Nepal Prime Minister K.P. Sharma Oli's visit to China in March 2016 is a message to India that Nepal has a viable option in mobilising support from China to counter any pressure generated from India. Mr. Oli concluded 10 important agreements and Memoranda of Understanding (MoU) covering fields of transit and trade, connectivity and infrastructure, energy exploration and storage, banking and education. It is evident that the new government in Nepal ignored India's concerns and advice and has blamed India for encouraging disturbances in the Terai and interfering in Nepal's internal affairs. There was also confusion regarding India's priorities i.e., an inclusive constitution addressing Madhes concerns or an accommodation of Hindutva and monarchical preferences or perhaps both. [23]

The ill-conceived diplomatic moves India made in response to Nepal's constitution and the Madhes agitation or resorting to pushing for a Hindu State agenda and revival of the monarchy in Nepal, popular with some sections of India's ruling party, to contain Chinese influence, will prove counter productive. [24] While the long-term objective of India should be to address the changing political narrative in Nepal, our present challenge is to recover lost political ground so that India can play the role of a trusted and irreplaceable interlocutor, between the two sides in Nepal but without resorting to micro management. India has to sit up and take a serious note of the Chinese push into South Asia, which is not simply limited to Nepal but covers all other neighbours as well. If India's smaller neighbours (as was the recent case with Nepal) perceive the outcomes of their relationship with her (India) as unequal or unfair, then cooperation will be difficult to secure, defeating the realisation of a South Asian 'commons'. [25]

Conclusions

The anti-Rana revolution of 1951, the success of UCPN (Maoists) in 2008, and the adoption of new Constitution in September 2015 and the Madhesi agitation against it, are all major landmarks in Nepal's political evolution which influenced the content and contours of Indo-Nepal relations. It is a well established truism that the bilateral relations between the two countries has been governed by treaties which are now outdated. If mutually beneficial developments are to take place, a sea change in the approach and attitudes of both countries, therefore, must occur. Nepal has to evolve a broad policy for India backed by a strong national consensus to maintain a long-term strategic relationship. Instead of using pressure tactics, India should help the Nepali leadership to sort out issues related to Madhes and Janjatis and engage with Nepal as a sovereign entity. India's conventional approach to improving bilateral relations may not work in the given context. India needs to pay due respect to the democratic aspirations of the Nepalese people, even if this does not corroborate well with India's perceived interests. [26]

The changing political dynamics and elite orientation in Nepal may not remain the same. Hence, the Indian mindset needs to be changed for a better understanding of the emerging trends in bilateral relations. India baiting from the side of the Nepali politicians and India's old mindset that Nepal should always remain a pliant state may not work in the changing regional and global context. [27] The so called Chinese influence on Nepal is to be dealt with diplomacy based on mutual understanding and mutual benefit in trade and security. India needs to change its diplomatic posture from a hardline position to quiet and creative initiatives where it can nudge both the marginalised and the dominant governing elites in Nepal to engage with each other meaningfully to work out credible and lasting compromises. A democratic federal Republic of Nepal will be a good neighbour to India, than a monarchy in the 21st century.

Endnotes

1. Pandey, Nishchal Nath (2010), "New Nepal: The Fault Lines", Sage Publications, p. 104.
2. Nepal's 2.5 million population deeply suffers from acute poverty. The country is rich in natural resources, as 17 percent land is worth farming. However, 80 percent of the adult population is associated with agriculture, 17 percent is with services and only 4 percent with the industry. The population growth rate annually is 2.29 and per capita income is US$ 250 per annum. Around 60 percent of the adult population is illiterate.
3. Rao, Chandramouleswara V. (2005), "Indo-Nepal Relations: A Historical Perspective", in M.D. Dharmadasani (ed.), 'Role of Japan and Nepal in Asian Politics', Gyan Publishng House, New Delhi. p. 81.
4. Singh, Amresh Kumar (2005), "Nepal's Political Security Relations with Special Reference to India", in M.D. Dhararmdasai (ed.), 'Role of Japan and Nepal in Asian Politics', Gyan Publishing House, New Delhi, p. 86.
5. B.P. Koirala of the Congress party was sworn in as Nepal's first

democratically elected Prime Minister in 1959. But King Mahendra engineered a royal coup soon after. B.P. Koirala spent seven years in prison and then went back in exile in Bihar and Uttar Pradesh. When Emergency was declared in India in 1975, he went back.

6. Khand, Jitendra Dhoj (2005), "Nepal's Political Security Relations with India, in M.D. Dharamdasani (ed)., 'Role of Japan and Nepal in Asian Politics", Gyan Publishing House, New Delhi, p. 59.
7. Khadka. N (1997), "Foreign Aid and Foreign Policy: Major Powers and Nepal", Vikas Publishing House, New Delhi, p. 231.
8. Muni, S.D. (1992), "India and Nepal: A Changing Relationship", Konark Publishers, New Delhi, p. 60.
9. Ramana, P.V. (2007), "PWG Naxal-Nepal Maoists Nexus", accessed at: http://www.orfonline.org.
10. *The Hindu,* May 10, 2009.
11. Singh, Amresh Kumar (2005), "Nepal's Political Security Relations with Special Reference to India", in M.D. Dhararmdasai (ed.), 'Role of Japan and Nepal in Asian Politics', Gyan Publishing House, New Delhi. p. 87.
12. Baral, Lok Raj (1992), "India-Nepal Relations: Continuity and Change", *Asian Survey,* Vol. XXXII (9), September, p. 816.
13. The seven party alliance included the Nepali Congress, CPN(UML), Jana Morcha Nepal, NWPP, ULF, NSP (Anandadevi) and the NSP (AD).
14. Mishra, Atul (2008), "Theorising State Sovereignty in South Asia", *Economic and Political Weekly,* Vol. XLIII (40), October 4-10, p. 69.
15. *The Hindu,* August 23, 2009.
16. Varadarajan, Siddharth (2009), "India's Nepal Policy in Disarray", *The Hindu,* May 7.
17. Adhikari, Aditya (2013), "Nepal: The Discontents after the Revolution", *Economic and Political Weekly*, Vol XLXVIII (7), February 16, pp. 27-29.
18. Lal, C.K. (2014), "Rightward Drift in Nepal", *Economic and Political Weekly,* Vol. XLIX (4), January 24.
19. Shreshta, Shyam (2014), "Maoist Defeat in Nepal: The Price of a Missed Opportunity", *Economic and Political Weekly,* Vol. XLIX (4), January 25.
20. 9.5 million citizens participated in the Constituent Assembly

elections of November 2013, making up fully 78 percent of registered voters. Of the 601 assembly members, 335 were placed through proportional representations and 240 were directly elected. 92 percent of the Constituent Assembly members endorsed the Constitution.

21. The 12 point agreement finally became an 8 point agreement which included framing of an interim constitution, establishment of an interim government, which would take up the task to conducting elections to the Constituent Assembly, issues related to the disarming of the Maoist force, the future of Maoist army and peace-building.
22. Dixit, Kanak Mani (2015), "Apply Panchaseel on Nepal", *The Hindu*, September 24.
23. Muni, S.D. (2015), "Nepal's New Constitution: Towards Progress or Chaos"?, *Economic and Political Weekly,* Vol. L(40), October 3, p. 18.
24. Muni, S.D. (2016), "No Zero Sum in the Great Game", *The Hindu,* March 28.
25. Rao, Nirupama (2016), "New, Strong and Clear Outreach", *The Hindu,* March 4.
26. Gautam Navlakha (2003), "From Battle of Arms to Battle of Ideas", *Economic and Political Weekly,* Vol. 38 (11), pp. 1032-1033.
27. Baral, Lok Raj (2012), "Nepal: Nation-State in the Wilderness, Managing State, Democracy and Geopolitics", Sage Publications, p. 225.

6

India-Central Asia Strategic Relations

Anurag Tripathi

After the collapse of the former Soviet Union, the Central Asian republics have engaged themselves in nation-building process and consolidation of their statehoods. In the meantime, they continue to face frightening socio-economic and security problems. Issues like border disputes, water security, environmental degradation, particularly shrinking of Aral Sea, migration and rise of Islamic extremism have posed significant challenge to the regional stability. The socio-economic development in Central Asian region is complex. Major world powers were involved in competition for influence in Central Asia, also known as the 'Great Game' politics. Similarly, American withdrawal from Afghanistan, would pose security challenge to these republics as the extremist elements will expand their horizons to Central Asia.

India and the Central Asia share a long history. Unfortunately the relationship, despite close historical and cultural contacts, has not progressed to the desired extent. The key restraint India faces is the lack of direct access to Central Asia. More importantly, the unstable situation in Afghanistan and Indo-Pak rivalry also is a stumbling block for smooth India-Central Asia relations.

In 2012, India has come up with a "Connect Central Asia Policy", which includes elements such as high level visits, strategic partnerships, comprehensive economic engagement, and partnership in the development of energy and natural resources. There is a vast scope for furthering bilateral ties in education and English language teaching from schools to universities, healthcare, tourism, agriculture and agro-processing industries, pharmaceuticals and drug manufacturing, textiles, petrochemicals, mining, military cooperation and cadre training, and other allied fields. The implementation of the policy needs to be speeded up. A good strategic relationship between India and Central Asia will provide more economic engagement.

Background

After the disintegration of the former Soviet Union, the Central Asian countries of Kazakhstan, Kyrgyzstan, Tajikistan, Turkmenistan and Uzbekistan have engaged themselves in nation-building process and consolidation of their statehoods. In the meantime, they continue to face frightening socio-economic and security problems. Issues like border disputes, water security, environmental degradation, particularly shrinking of Aral Sea, and migration and rise of Islamic extremism have posed significant challenge to the regional stability. The socio-economic development in Central Asian region is complex and mixed. Kazakhstan is doing better than others because of its vast mineral resources. Kyrgyzstan and Tajikistan lag behind the others in socio-economic development. Uzbekistan and Turkmenistan remain as closed and controlled societies. [1]

Historically, Central Asian region has been an arena of "great game" between Russia and Britain. The modern version of "great game" is being played out even today among Russia, China, US, Turkey, Iran, Europe, EU, Japan, Pakistan, India, and Afghanistan because of economic and security interests. In order to maximize their geopolitical advantage and also to ensure their national interests, the Central Asian countries have also engaged with the rest of the world through their active policies in the international arena. [2]

India and Central Asia

India and the Central Asian region share long historical, cultural and economic relations. Through the Silk Route, both regions were connected with each other. It was not only business but a lot of other things like culture and beliefs, which also connected them. For example, Buddhism, having its origin and growth in India, was welcomed in Central Asia, and similarly, Sufiana culture popular in India have their connections with that region. [3] An evidence of the spread of Buddhism is a twelve meter long Buddha statue in Tajikistan, and the massive statues of Buddha at Bamiyan in Afghanistan.

Post-Independence India's relations with Central Asia were shaped by Delhi's closeness to the Union of Soviet Socialist Republics (USSR). Constrained by its ties to the Soviet Union, as well as by a general inward looking focus during the Cold War period, India's presence in the region was mostly limited to cultural exchanges. [4] After the collapse of the former Soviet Union in 1991, India was the only non-communist nation, which made diplomatic relations with the Central Asian countries. For example, in 1987, India was one of the first countries to open a consulate in what later on became Uzbekistan's capital Tashkent. This Indian consulate in Tashkent had jurisdiction over the Kazakh, Kyrgyz, Tajik, Turkmen and Uzbek Soviet Socialist Republics. [5] Post-Cold War, India's efforts to engage with Central Asian region had mainly two primary concerns: first, securing and diversifying India's energy supplies in order to sustain economic growth; and second, keeping a check on the rise of radical Islamist groups that may pose a threat to India's security. [6] This article has been structured under three broad areas:

1. India's strategic interests in the region.
2. Opportunities in India-Central Asia relations.
3. Challenges in India-Central Asia relations.

The Central Asian countries have a combined land area of 3,994,300 square kilometres. [7] The region also derives its strategic significance from the fact that it borders two of the five permanent members of the United Nations Security Council—China and Russia—whereas it also borders or near borders with four nuclear powers, Russia, China, Pakistan and India. Despite their desire to preserve their identity they are also inclined to forge logistical linkages with the outer world. [8] From the last decade, India started recognizing the Central Asian region because of its geostrategic and geoeconomic importance. India introduced 'Look North Policy' for Central Asian States in the 1990s. During a visit to Turkmenistan during September 19-21, 1995, [9] Prime Minister, P.V. Narasimha Rao, made it amply clear that 'for India', Central Asia is an area of high priority, where we aim to stay engaged far into the future. [10] However, while a 'grand strategic vision' may not be visible, there has been a pattern to India's position with regard to Central Asia. The key constraints India faces in Central Asia are the following:

- Lack of direct access to Central Asia.
- The unstable situation in Afghanistan.
- Highly problematic India-Pakistan relations.

Following constraints have deprived India from the benefit of relations with Central Asia. If TAPI pipeline (Turkmenistan-Afghanistan-Pakistan-India) materializes, no doubt it would be a game changer in India-Central Asia relations. However, despite some positive developments like the signing of an inter-governmental agreement, realization of TAPI is still some distance away. [11]

In June 2012, New Delhi launched a new 'Connect Central Asia' policy. The aims of the new policy are to promote pro-active engagement with the five states, both bilaterally and multilaterally. On June 12, 2012 India's Minister of State for External Affairs Shri E. Ahamed gave a keynote address at First India-Central Asia Dialogue. He outlined some of the elements of India's 'Connect Central Asia' policy as follows:

1. India will continue to build on our strong political relations through the exchange of high level visits. Its leaders will continue to interact closely both in bilateral and multilateral fora.
2. India will strengthen its strategic and security cooperation. India already has strategic partnerships in place with some Central Asian countries. In focus, will be military training,

joint research, counter-terrorism coordination and close consultations on Afghanistan.

3. India will step up multilateral engagement with Central Asian partners using the synergy of joint efforts through existing fora like the Shanghai Cooperation Organisation, Eurasian Economic Community (EEC) and the Custom Union. India has already proposed a Comprehensive Economic Cooperation Agreement to integrate its markets with the unifying Eurasian space.
4. India looks to Central Asia as a long-term partner in energy, and natural resources. Central Asia possesses large cultivable tracts of land and it sees potential for India to cooperate in production of profitable crops with value addition.
5. The medical field is another area that offers huge potential for cooperation. India is ready to extend cooperation by setting up civil hospitals/clinics in Central Asia.
6. India's higher education system delivers at a fraction of the fees charged by Western universities. Keeping this in mind, India would like to assist in the setting up of a Central Asian University in Bishkek that could come up as a centre of excellence to impart world class education in areas like information technology, management, philosophy and languages.
7. India is working on setting up a Central Asian e-network with its hub in India, to deliver, tele-education and tele-medicine connectivity, linking all the five Central Asian States.
8. Indian companies can showcase their capability in the construction sector and build world class structures at competitive rates. Central Asian countries, especially Kazakhstan, have almost limitless reserves of iron ore and coal, as well as abundant cheap electricity. India can help set up several medium size steel rolling mills, producing its requirement of specific products.
9. As for land connectivity, India has reactivated the International North-South Transport Corridor (INSTC).

India and Central Asian nations need to join our efforts to discuss ways to bridge the missing links in the Corridor at the earliest and also work on other connecting spurs along the route.

10. Absence of a viable banking infrastructure in the region is a major barrier to trade and investment. Indian banks can expand their presence if they see a favourable policy environment.
11. India will jointly work to improve air connectivity between the countries. India is one of the biggest markets for outbound travellers estimated at US$ 21 billion in 2011. Many countries have opened tourist offices in India to woo Indian tourists. Central Asian countries could emerge as attractive holiday destinations for tourists and even for the Indian film industry which likes to depict exotic foreign locales in its films.
12. Connections between our peoples are the most vital linkages to sustain our deep engagement. I would particularly like to emphasise exchanges between youth and the future leaders of India and Central Asia. India already has a robust exchange of students. India will encourage regular exchanges of scholars, academics, civil society and youth delegations to gain deeper insights into each other's cultures. [12]

This signalled that India would seek to build stronger political relations and strengthen strategic and security cooperation with Central Asian states.

Importantly, India should realize the potential of Chabahar Port in Iran. The significance of Chabahar Port is that it will facilitate a transit route to land-locked Afghanistan. Despite direct road links, Pakistan does not allow transit facility from India to Afghanistan. Therefore, connectivity through the Chabahar Port could become an important route linking India to Afghanistan and Central Asia. India will require making substantial investments in Iran to make the INSTC as well as Chabahar Port to provide short and effective access to Central Asia.

Recent visit of Prime Minister Modi in June and July 2015 to Central Asia comes in the backdrop of ominous events having potential of making significant impact on India's national security interests as well as changing equations in international relations. [13] The Modi government could now re-examine the scope of the Connect Central Asia policy in the context of the new strategic environment.

India already cooperates bilaterally with Kazakhstan on nuclear energy, space flight and cyber-security; with Uzbekistan on joint military training exercises and building electricity infrastructure; and with Tajikistan on counter-terrorism and hydropower. The 'Connect Central Asia' policy announced in Bishkek in June 2012 added only marginally to the existing menu of activities, but did at least describe the vision in one frame, in terms accessible to would be investors from India. The policy included ambitions for establishing universities, hospitals and information technology centres, an e-network in telemedicine connecting India to Central Asia, facilitation of joint commercial ventures, improved civilian air connectivity with Delhi to boost trade and tourism, and joint scientific research and partnerships in defence and security. Till date, direct air links and new commercial ventures illustrate some progress; security and defence partnerships were already established and have continued. [14]

Challenges and Opportunities

Energy: Energy is a prime concern of Indian policy makers in future. India's dependence on imported oil is projected to escalate from the current level of 83.5 percent as of June 20, 2014 to more than 90 percent by 2030. [15] Central Asia has an estimated four percent (270-360 trillion cubic feet) of the world's gas reserves; its oil reserves are pegged at 2.7 percent (13-15 billion barrels). [16] The energy resources of Central Asia, including the Caspian Sea region, will play an important role in India's energy strategy. Central Asian oil and gas are of high quality and largely untapped. The investment environment is open and friendly. In addition, Central Asia is relatively more stable than the Middle East and African energy rich countries. [17]

Prime Minister Narendra Modi's recent visits in five Central Asian countries are significant because India is yet to achieve a strategic comeback in Eurasia's energy heartland—India will need to become a key player in Central Asian energy markets. Already, the national oil companies of the two counties, ONGC Videsh Ltd. (OVL) of India and KazMunaiGas of Kazakhstan are engaged in Kazakhstan's Satpayev oil exploration project. The OVL had aimed to buy American company Conoco Philip's 8.4 percent share valued at US$ 5 billion in the Kashagan oil field. [18] On July 7, 2015, Prime Minister Narendra Modi and Kazakhstan premier Karim Massimov launched the first exploratory drilling of the Satpayev oil block by India's OVL and KazMunaiGaz. [19] Significantly, enriched uranium is another important concern for India. All the Central Asian countries have enough amounts of uranium reserves to fulfil India's nuclear energy need. In this regard, Kazakh uranium mining company KazAtomProm has signed a contract with India's Department of Atomic Energy (DAE) to supply 5,000 tonnes of uranium over the next four years. [20]

Security: Today, there are mounting security concerns in Central Asia and South Asia over rising cross-border and state sponsored terrorism; religious extremism/political Islam and ethnic unrest, radiating out of Afghanistan and Pakistan. [21] Terrorism is gaining prominence in the range of non-traditional threats in both the regions. India is facing cross-border terrorism sponsored by Pakistan in Jammu and Kashmir (J&K) and Central Asia in Uzbekistan, Kyrgyzstan and Tajikistan. Significantly, according to the Central Intelligence Agency (CIA), IS militants in Iraq and Syria now have about 20,000 to 31,500 fighters on the ground. In June 2014, *The Economist* reported that "ISIS may have up to 6,000 fighters in Iraq and 3,000-5,000 in Syria, including perhaps 3,000 foreigners; nearly a thousand are reported to hail from Chechnya and perhaps 500 or so more from France, Britain and elsewhere in Europe".

According to *The New York Times*, in September, there were more than 2,000 Europeans and 100 Americans among ISIS's foreign fighters. Tunisia has sent 2,400-3,000 foreign fighters to the Islamic State, more than any other nation. According to the media reports, there are about "250 Kazakh citizens, 100 Kyrgyz, 190 Tajiks, 500 Uzbeks, and about 360 Turkmens fighting alongside IS extremists", with Turkmenistan, Kyrgyzstan being the most vulnerable to IS influence, especially via Ferghana Valley. However, these numbers are difficult to confirm. [22] Significantly, Central Asian militants are already fighting in Afghanistan and the Federally Administered Tribal Areas (FATA) and Khyber Pakhtunkhwa provinces of Pakistan for the past few years. Continuous drone strikes by the United States in Pakistan and militant operations in Afghanistan have destroyed the militants' bases. After such continuous operations in both the countries, several Central Asian militants have chosen to travel to J&K. On October 18, 2014, security forces arrested an Al-Badr (group active in Afghanistan) militant identified as Irfan Ahmad Bhat alias Irra from Sopore area in Baramullah District in North Kashmir.

India has a vital interest in the security and political stability of this region. Obviously, given the Kashmir angle, India cannot be walled off from the political developments which take place in the Central Asian region. Violent turbulence in Central Asian states is affecting India negatively. On the other hand, instability in Afghanistan has also adversely influenced peace and security in our region. Afghanistan and Pakistan continue to be the key actors creating destabilisation in Central Asia as well as in India.

Drug Trafficking: Drug trafficking is one of the main security threats for India in the context of Central Asia. According to the World Drug Report 2011, Afghanistan has been the largest opium producer of the world. [23] Because of its geographical proximity to Afghanistan, Central Asia has become a hub of drugs and narcotics transportation. The emergence of Central Asia as a transit route for drugs is directly linked to the growing spread of drug addiction amongst the Central Asian people and funding of terrorist organisations which in turn are used against India. [24]

Commercial Opportunities: Central Asia offers a relatively untapped market for Indian consumer goods, especially as consumers in the region have little to choose from between highly priced, imported Western products and cheap but low quality Chinese manufactured goods that have flooded the region. [25] There is a vast scope for furthering bilateral ties in education and English language teaching from schools to universities, healthcare, tourism, agriculture and agro-processing industries, pharmaceuticals and drug manufacturing, textiles, petrochemicals, mining, military cooperation and cadre training, and other allied fields.

The Indian government has set up intergovernmental commissions for trade, economic, scientific and technical cooperation with all the Central Asian countries, and these have been meeting regularly. Furthermore, there have been improvements in terms of cooperation in the banking sector. Canara Bank has links with the Commercial Bank for Foreign Economic Affairs of Tajikistan. State Bank of India has links with the Turan-Alem Bank of Kazakhstan, the Commercial Bank of Kyrgyzstan, the National Bank of Tajikistan, the State Bank for Foreign Economic Affairs of Turkmenistan and the National Bank for Foreign Economic Activity of Uzbekistan.

In 2003, the Indian Ministry of Commerce launched a programme named 'Focus CIS'. India has also signed many agreements with these countries for technical and economic cooperation under the ITEC. Thus far, thousands of candidates from Central Asia have come to India under the programme in such disciplines as diplomacy, banking, finance, trade, management and small industry promotion. [26] Although the volume of overall Indian trade with the region remains low, an emergent trend between 2008 and 2013 has been the increase in the export of Indian pharmaceuticals to the region.

India's Trade with CAR Countries, 1996-2012

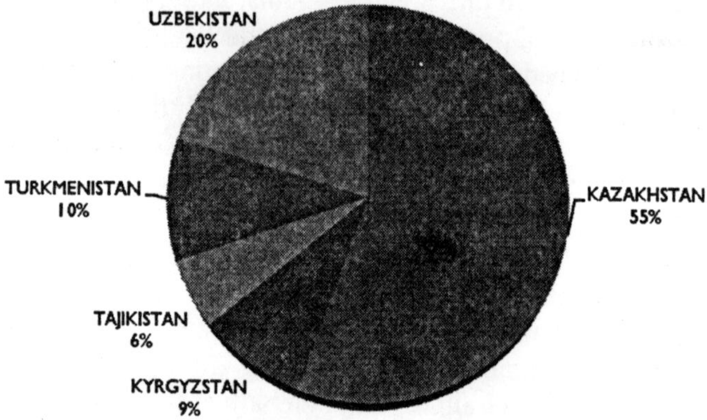

Source: Data collated and calculated by Indian Development Cooperation Research, based on data from EXIM Bank 1996-2012, Ministry of Trade and Commerce, Government of India.

Although in economic terms, India and Central Asia do not share much satisfactory relationship, India has somewhat meagre presence in the Central Asian energy sector and growing presence in the field of pharmaceuticals. The implementation of the policy needs to be speeded up. A good strategic relationship between India and Central Asia will provide more economic engagement.

Shanghai Co-operation Organisation (SCO)

India was on July 10, 2015, accepted as a full member of the Shanghai Cooperation Organisation (SCO), a six-member regional grouping, to which Prime Minister Narendra Modi offered to work in combating terror and boosting trade by easing barriers. India, which has had an observer status for the past 10 years, will technically become a member by next year after completion of certain procedures.

The SCO has now emerged as a major geostrategic, security and economic initiative in entire Eurasia. It would also facilitate India to counter Pakistan's anti-India propaganda and guarantee its economic participation with the greater Central Asian region.

Central Asia's geostrategic location and its rich energy resources offer much reason for intensive engagement with the region nonetheless; there are two major challenges that need to be addressed, like lack of direct geographical access and rise of Islam extremism in the region that has been egged on by support from Wahhabi elements of Saudi Arabia and Pakistan.

To this effect, it has used the Kashmir issue, albeit with limited success, by portraying it as a case of the oppression of Muslims at the hands of the 'Hindu-dominated' Indian state. [27] India's strategic interests at stake in the region, make it imperative for the country to evolve a clear policy, capable of addressing the existing as well as potential challenges that may arise in the future.

India has sought to overcome the lack of geographical access to Central Asia by developing the Chabahar Port in Iran which will provide a transit route to land-locked Afghanistan and Central Asia. In the economic field also, India could deepen its footprint by effectively building on its strengths in IT, banking and the small and medium-scale enterprise sectors.

Conclusion

Because of the geographical proximity and common history and cultural affinity, India and Central Asia are natural allies. India's policy towards Central Asia has been ad hoc in nature and reactive rather than being pro-active toward development.

In order to avoid reactiveness and to be pro-active, India should define its position and priorities in the region. India needs to pursue serious and active bilateral, regional and multilateral agreements to promote security in the region. Because of its soft power image, India can do what it wants in the region.

Endnotes

1. Gupta, Arvind (2014), "India and Central Asia: Need for a Pro-active Approach" *IDSA,* accessed at: http://www.idsa.in/policybrief/IndiaandCentralAsiaagupta_1410 13.
2. Ibid.
3. Zafar, Athar (2015), "India-Central Asia: Finding New Synergies for Greater Engagement" *ICWA,* accessed at: http://www.icwa.in/pdfs/PB/2014/IndiaCentralAsiaPB09072015 .pdf.
4. Campbell, Ivan (2013), "India's Role and Interests in Central Asia", *Safer World,* accessed at: http://www.indias-role-and-interests-in-central-asia.pdf.
5. Asoke, Mukerji, "India, Central Asia and the new Silk Road", discussion meeting, July 10, 2012, Arundel House, London, accessed at: http://www.iiss.org/en/events/events/archive/2012-4a49/july-70c4/india-central-asia-and-the-new-silk-road-e4d1.
6. Campbell, Ivan (2013), "India's Role and Interests in Central Asia", *Safer World,* accessed at: file:///C:/Users/anurag/Downloads/indias-role-and-interests-in-central-asia.pdf.
7. "Central Asia: General Information", *Advantour*, accessed at: http://www.advantour.com/central-asia/index.htm.
8. Khawaja, Asma Shakir (2014), "The Geo-Strategic Dimension of India and Central Asia Bilateral Relations: An Analysis", *FRPC Journal,* accessed at: http://www.fprc.in/pdf/J-10.pdf.
9. "India-Turkmenistan Relations" (2014), accessed at: http://www.mea.gov.in/Portal/ForeignRelation/Turkmenistan_July_2014.pdf.
10. Pradhan, Ramakrushna (2015), "India's Soft Power in Central Asia: Why it Must Act on the Look North Policy", *Mainstream,* Vol. LIII, No. 29, New Delhi, July 11, 2015.
11. Gupta, Arvind (2014), "India and Central Asia: Need for a Pro-

active Approach", *IDSA,* accessed at: http://www.idsa.in/policybrief/IndiaandCentralAsia_agupta_141013.

12. "India's 'Connect Central Asia' Policy" (2012), keynote address by MoS Shri E. Ahamed at First India-Central Asia Dialogue, *MEA,* accessed at: http://www.mea.gov.in/Speeches-Statements.htm?dtl/19791/Keynote+address+by+MOS+Shri+E+Ahamed+at+First+IndiaCentral+Asia+Dialogue.
13. Soti, Divya Kumar (2015), "Modi's Central Asia Visit: Russia Could Welcome the India Factor", *South Asia Monitor,* accessed at: http://southasiamonitor.org/detail.php?type=sl&nid=12620.
14. Daultrey, S. (2015), "Modi's Central Asia Visit: New Opportunities, New Approach", *South Asia Monitor,* accessed at: http://southasiamonitor.org/detail.php?type=sl&nid=12748.
15. TERI (2012), "National Energy Map for India: Technology Vision 2030", *The Energy Research Institute*, New Delhi.
16. Sharma, Raghav (2009), "India in Central Asia: The Road Ahead", *Institute of Peace and Conflict Studies,* special report, No. 63, January, p. 4.
17. Pradhan, Ramakrushna (2015), "India's Soft Power in Central Asia: Why it Must Act on the Look North Policy", *Mainstream*, Vol. LIII, No. 29, New Delhi, July 11, 2015.
18. Zafar, Athar (2014), "India-Kazakhstan: Finding New Synergies", *ICWA,* accessed at: http://www.icwa.in/pdfs/VP/2014/VPFindingNewSynergies.pdf.
19. "India, Kazakhstan Launch First Drilling at Satpayev Oil Block", July 7, 2015, *Indian Express*, accessed at: http://www.newindianexpress.com/world/India-Kazakhstan-Launch-First-Drilling-at-Satpayev-Oil-Block/2015/07/07/article2907527.ece.
20. "Kazakhstan Agrees to Supply Uranium to India, July 8, 2015, *World Nuclear News,* accessed at: http://www.world-nuclear-news.org/UF-Kazakhstan-agrees-to-supply-uranium-to-India-0807156.html.
21. Roy, Meena Singh, "India's Interests in Central Asia", *IDSA,* accessed at: http://www.idsa-india.org/an-mar-9.01.html.

22. Tripathi, Anurag (2014), "Islamic State Attracting Central Asia Youth" *South Asia Monitor,* accessed at: http://southasiamonitor.org/detail.php?type=gwatch&nid=9474.
23. World Drug Report, 2011.
24. Pradhan, Ramakrushna (2015), "India's Soft Power in Central Asia: Why it Must Act on the Look North Policy", *Mainstream*, Vol. LIII, No. 29, New Delhi, July 11, 2015.
25. Campbell, Ivan (2013), "India's Role and Interests in Central Asia", *Safer World,* accessed at: file:///C:/Users/anurag/Downloads/indias-role-and-interests-in-central-asia.pdf.
26. Pradhan, Ramakrushna (2015), "India's Soft Power in Central Asia: Why it Must Act on the Look North Policy", *Mainstream*, Vol. LIII, No. 29, New Delhi, July 11, 2015.
27. Sharma, Raghav (2009), "India in Central Asia: The Road Ahead", *Institute of Peace and Conflict Studies,* Special Report, No. 63, January.

References

Asoke, Mukerji, "India, Central Asia and the New Silk Road", discussion meeting, July 10, 2012, Arundel House, London, accessed at: http://www.iiss.org/en/events/events/archive/2012-4a49/july-70c4/india-central-asia-and-the-new-silk-road-e4d1.

Campbell, Ivan (2013), "India's Role and Interests in Central Asia", *Safer World,* accessed at: C:/Users/anurag/Downloads/indias-role-and-interests-in-central-asia.pdf.

"Central Asia: General Information", *Advantour*, accessed at: http://www.advantour.com/central-asia/index.htm.

Daultrey, S. (2015), "Modi's Central Asia Visit: New Opportunities, New Approach", *South Asia Monitor,* accessed at: http://southasiamonitor.org/detail.php?type=sl&nid=12748.

Gupta, Arvind (2014), "India and Central Asia: Need for a Pro-active Approach", *IDSA,* accessed at: http://www.idsa.in/policybrief/IndiaandCentralAsia_agupta_141013.

"India's 'Connect Central Asia' Policy (2012)", keynote address by MoS Shri E. Ahamed at First India-Central Asia Dialogue", *MEA,* accessed at:

http://www.mea.gov.in/Speeches-Statements.htm?dtl/19791/Keynote+address+by+MOS+Shri+E+Ahamed+at+First+IndiaCentral+Asia+Dialogue.

"India, Kazakhstan Launch First Drilling at Satpayev Oil Block", July 7, 2015, *Indian Express*, accessed at: http://www.newindianexpress.com/world/India-Kazakhstan-Launch-First-Drilling-at-Satpayev-Oil-Block/2015/07/07/article2907527.ece.

"India-Turkmenistan Relations" (2014), accessed at: http://www.mea.gov.in/Portal/ForeignRelation/Turkmenistan_July_2014.pdf.

"Kazakhstan Agrees to Supply Uranium to India", July 8, 2015, *World Nuclear News,* accessed at: http://www.world-nuclear-news.org/UF-Kazakhstan-agrees-to-supply-uranium-to-India-0807156.html.

Khawaja Asma Shakir (2014), "The Geo-Strategic Dimension of India and Central Asia Bilateral Relations: An Analysis", *FRPC Journal,* accessed at: http://www.fprc.in/pdf/J-10.pdf.

Pradhan, Ramakrushna (2014), "India's Soft Power in Central Asia: Why it Must Act on the Look North Policy", *Mainstream*, Vol. LIII, No. 29, New Delhi, July 11, 2015.

Roy, Meena Singh, "India's Interests in Central Asia", *IDSA,* accessed at: http://www.idsa-india.org/an-mar-9.01.html.

Sharma, Raghav (2009), "India in Central Asia: The Road Ahead", *Institute of Peace and Conflict Studies,* special report, No. 63, January, p. 4.

Soti, Divya Kumar (2015), "Modi's Central Asia Visit: Russia Could Welcome the India Factor", *South Asia Monitor,* accessed at: http://southasiamonitor.org/detail.php?type=sl&nid=12620.

TERI (2012), "National Energy Map for India: Technology Vision 2030", *The Energy Research Institute*, New Delhi.

Tripathi, Anurag (2014), "Islamic State Attracting Central Asia Youth", *South Asia Monitor,* accessed at: http://southasiamonitor.org/detail.php?type=gwatch&nid=9474.

World Drug Report, 2011.

Zafar, Athar (2015), "India-Central Asia: Finding New Synergies for Greater Engagement", *ICWA,* accessed at: http://www.icwa.in/pdfs

/PB/2014/IndiaCentralAsiaPB09072015.pdf.

Zafar, Athar (2014), "India-Kazakhstan: Finding New Synergies", *ICWA,* accessed at: http://www.icwa.in/pdfs/VP/2014/VPFindingNewSynergies.pdf.

7

India and European Union: Security and Strategic Aspects

B. Krishnamurthy and Vijayata Rani

Section I

India was one among the few countries to maintain close relationship with the European Community (EC) since its inception. The Cooperation Agreement on Partnership and Development signed by India and the European Union (EU) in 1993, signified a more equal relationship between them. The first-ever India-EU summit meeting was held on June 28, 2000 in Lisbon and this Summit was the manifestation of the EU's political will to engage India as a major player in an emerging multipolar world.

Moreover, it is considered as a milestone in India-EU relations and an event of greater significance for India both in symbol and in substance. The EU used to hold such summit meetings with the US, Russia, Canada, China and Japan alone earlier and India became the sixth country. All these clearly show that the EU treats India differentially from its South Asian neighbours and considers it as the primary interlocutor in this region. In its 'concentric circle' [1] of external relations, India stands at par with China and Japan in Asia.

In their Joint Declaration at the end of the inaugural session at the Lisbon summit, EU and India announced their resolve to "build a new strategic partnership in the 21st century founded on shared values and aspirations characterized by enhanced and multi-faceted cooperation". It was stated that this was an apt moment for launching "a new phase of constructive and mutually beneficial partnership" in the wake of the "enhanced and sustained growth" of India and integration and enlargement of the EU.

By mid-2003, Javier Solana, the then High Representative for Common Foreign and Security Policy, in his effort to chart out future course of the Union in its external relations, came up with the European Security Strategy (ESS) and it was approved by the leaders of the member states of the Union in December 2003. He not only enumerated the threats faced by Europe but also put forth strategies to face these challenges squarely. One of the strategies advocated by Solana was to develop strategic partnerships with the US, Russia, Japan, China, Canada and India. [2] It is significant to note that the ESS, which is based on the concept of comprehensive security, identified India as part of EU's global security strategy and considered the country as one among the 'key' strategic partners. [3]

Subsequently, India and the EU signed a strategic partnership in June 2004. The communication issued by the European Commission in this regard proposed to develop such a partnership with India in four key areas: (a) cooperation in international fora on conflict prevention, the fight against terrorism and non-proliferation of weapons of mass destruction; (b) economic partnership through strategic policy and sectoral dialogues; (c) development cooperation, and (d) fostering intellectual and cultural exchanges. The EU also sought to intensify and broaden political dialogue. Moreover, the partnership suggested that 'the EU must help India [to achieve] social and economic cohesion [because] poverty is still widespread, unemployment or underemployment is high and vast disparities persist'. The EU, thus, intended on encouraging India 'to achieve greater convergence' with international standards. [4]

The India-EU Strategic Partnership was endorsed and launched on November 8, 2004 on the eve of the Fifth India-EU Summit at The Hague. The Joint Press Statement issued on the occasion clearly brought out the intention of the parties to have "dialogue on disarmament and non-proliferation; regular exchange of views on possibilities for co-operation on themes like resolution of conflicts, peace operations and reconstruction". [5] Subsequently, at the India-EU Summit at New Delhi on September 7, 2005, a comprehensive and forward looking Joint Action Plan (JAP) was adopted as an evolving roadmap outlining concrete actions to operationalise and strengthen the partnership. The JAP addressed five global issues on which the EU and India entertained divergent opinions. Under the title of 'deepening political dialogue and cooperation', these issues cover democracy and human rights, multilateralism, conflict prevention and post-conflict reconstruction, disarmament and non-proliferation and terrorism. The JAP proposed a wide range of supporting activities in the areas of political, economic, and development cooperation.

The Joint Political Declaration on the India-EU strategic partnership issued at Brussels on September 7, 2005, was deemed to be the "starting point" of a joint reflection that would lead to "a firm and visible upgrading" of the EU-India relationship, from the existing dialogue between "good friends" to "a truly strategic partnership" between two major players. India and the EU, as the largest democracies in the world, sought to pursue economic progress and prosperity for their peoples in a peaceful, stable and secure global environment.

They also pronounced their determination to establish an EU-India security dialogue on global and regional security issues, disarmament and non-proliferation; to launch an India-EU Initiative on Clean Development and Climate Change, with the aim of promoting cleaner technologies and their use and to cooperate in the energy sector to develop more efficient, cleaner and alternative energy chains and work to secure India's membership in the ITER nuclear fusion project. [6]

The JAP of 2005 was reviewed in order to set new goals and guidelines for the partnership and was updated in Marseilles summit held in 2008. 40-odd new activities in four areas—peace and comprehensive security, sustainable development, research and technology, and people-to-people and cultural exchanges—were added to the already existing activities. [7] The EU and India formally registered their determination 'to promote peace and comprehensive security' not only for the concerned parties but for the world at large.

Of late, it is widely believed that the strategic partnership between India and the EU turned out to be ineffective and failed to achieve something substantial, in spite of the potential behind the two powers as well as better prospects that the partnership enjoy. It is alleged that several factors caused such a setback and the main being reluctance on the part of the two powers to believe, behave and to treat each other as security and strategic actors of consequence at the global level. Mutual trust deficit and differentiation on the perception of strategic partnership and what is to be achieved by such an arrangement too remain yet another factor.

The present paper attempts to study and analyse how far the India-EU strategic partnership is effective and why it is being considered as ineffective; argues that the reluctance on the part of both the powers to present themselves as security and strategic actors of consequence result in such an ineffectiveness and suggests that both the partners should reenergise and revitalize their strategic partnership so as to make it more effective and delivering the desired outcomes.

Section II

Paul Kennedy delineated grand strategy as consisting of policies that reflect "the capacity of [a] nation's leaders to bring together all of the elements, both military and non-military, for the preservation and enhancement of [a] nation's long-term (that is, in wartime *and* peacetime) best interests". [8] The term 'strategic' is defined as anything relating to long-term interests and goals and as a natural corollary, a 'strategic partnership' relates to long-term shared interests and ways and means of achieving them. It is also expected to address political and security affairs effectively and in a regular and structured way. Since the late 1990s, the EU has signed and at present maintains strategic partnerships with key partners—Brazil, Canada, China, India, Japan, Mexico, Russia, South Africa, South Korea and the United States and with regions (especially Latin America). The strategic partnership with India is, thus, one among ten the Union has worldwide and one of four in Asia. [9]

Strategic partnerships are considered by the Europeans as a foreign policy concept as well as a tool to achieve the foreign policy goals and Renard is quite emphatic when he maintains that the strategic partnerships could become an important tool in shaping a multilateral order. [10] The ESS of 2003, was the first document to envision the strategic partnerships as a foreign policy tool and strategic partnerships with key global actors, was advocated as a mean to secure Europe and the world. Solana suggested that the EU should look to develop "strategic partnerships with all those who share our goals and values, and are prepared to act in their support". [11] Sharing the European goals and values and acting in their support was presented as criteria for signing and maintaining strategic partnerships with EU as a partner.

Renard and Biscop maintain that the motivations of the strategic partnerships that the EU signed with other key partners are the need to address the politico-economic developments in the international arena due to the emergence of the powers such as China and India; to provide an multilateral alternative for reinvigorating diplomacy in which bilateral approaches continue to dominate; and to assert its importance over the national diplomacies pursued by the member states. [12] Natalie Hess believes that the strategic partnerships have been an attempt by the EU institutions to raise the profile of the Union as an interesting interlocutor in the eyes of the emerging countries in comparison with its member states. [13] As such, the EU's strategic partnerships are "a necessary (sub-)strategy for the EU to cope successfully with the changing global order and to avoid global irrelevance" and "a blueprint for a smart use of the EU's power". [14]

The economic flipside of the strategic partnerships is seen as an attempt on the part of the EU to adapt its trade policy to the emergence of its partners in the economic sphere. The EU is expected to "take concrete steps to secure ambitious free trade agreements, secure greater market access for European businesses and deepen regulatory cooperation with major trade partners". [15] As such, trade enhancement benefiting the economic betterment of the Union seems to be the main objective of strategic partnerships. Anne Coulon categorically maintains that 'Rising India', has become an indispensable strategic partner for Europe due to its potential impact on the world economy, its role in G20 and WTO negotiations and especially due to the fact that it is the leader of developing and less developed countries. [16]

India is rated as pivotal partner by the Union, since the strategic partnership with it is quite important to cope with the contemporary global challenges and to achieve its core foreign policy objectives. The India-EU strategic partnership is being considered as essentially pivotal because it "can tip the international balance to the benefit or to the detriment of the EU depending on how we approach it". [17] In her speech on the BRICS and other emerging powers on February 1, 2012, Catherine Ashton, the then EU High Representative for Foreign Affairs and Security Policy, by way of acknowledging the importance of these emerging economies such as India stated that the EU needs "to invest in these countries as strategic partners in a very strong and dynamic, bilateral relationship [...] We need to do that because it is in our interest to do it". [18]

On the other hand, India has signed more than thirty strategic partnerships including the one with the EU and three of its member states—France (signed as early as 1998), Germany (2000) and the United Kingdom (2004), besides the

US, Russia and China. It considered its strategic partnerships with great and major powers, as a tool to enhance its standing in international politics and as a mechanism to enhance and ensure its security and strategic interests. For India, a strategic partnership with the EU, a regional economic grouping which is of late acquiring a political and strategic personality, complements and supplements its efforts to emerge as a major power in world politics, since it institutionalises a more productive, systematic and strategic multi-level dialogue with more concrete deliverables on a broader spectrum of issues.

Section III

The success of the Indian foreign policy in the context of India-EU strategic partnership can be measured in India's success in securing the European cooperation and assistance in achieving its foreign policy goals like recognition as a major power, positive and constructive reaction to its domestic problems, achievement of economic growth, poverty eradication, science and technology transfer and so on. Through its regular and constant negotiations and dialogues with the EU, India could achieve several positive impacts and to force the Union to reverse its earlier anti-Indian stands and pronouncements and to transform them into positive and constructive actions.

For instance, regarding the Kashmir issue and the Indo-Pakistan relations, the EU was lukewarm and wishy-washy for a couple of decades. Of late, the EU has taken a stand that Kashmir is an integral part of India and Lars-Olof Lindgren, the Swedish ambassador, who led the five-member fact-finding team to Srinagar in November 2006 maintained, "That is the opinion of the European Union. That is our opinion and that is the starting point of the discussion". [19] This pro-Indian stand also reflected in the EU Kashmir Report of 2006 titled "Kashmir: Present Situation and Future Prospects", of Baroness Emma Nicholson, Member of the European Parliament, the EU *rapporteur* and Vice Chair of the Foreign

Affairs Committee. The report was also highly critical of Pakistan's role in the Kashmir tangle and the situation in PoK. [20] Islamabad was particularly irked over the report's dismissal of calls for plebiscite to resolve the Kashmir issue. The original draft report had said that 'continuing calls for a plebiscite on the final status of Jammu and Kashmir are wholly out of step with the needs of the local people and thus damaging to their interests'. [21] As such, Nicolson's report proved itself to be "an extraordinarily pro-Indian document". [22]

In early 1990s, when the Europeans insisted on the inclusion of human rights clause in the India-EU Partnership Programme, the Indian Government opposed it tooth and nail. There was a delay of ten month in the signing of the Memorandum on Political and Economic Cooperation between India and the EU because of the latter's insistence on stipulating certain conditionalities on issues such as human rights and democracy and the Indian stand that "regardless of our credibility in these matters, we should not, even by implication, subject ourselves to external value judgments or certifications". [23] In the end, the Europeans had to relent. The fact that India is one among the top ten recipients of EC development cooperation assistance in 2004-05 clearly reflects "political priorities the Union attaches to its cooperation policy in its relationship with India". [24]

In realizing the Indian ambitions in the sphere of nuclear power programmes, the member states of the EU, especially France, helped India in the crucial hours of 1998 after its nuclear test by not supporting the sanctions regime imposed by the US. [25] In October 1998, the Union came out with a 'common position' aimed at promoting non-proliferation and confidence-building in South Asia—offered "financial and conceptual contributions" to initiatives for enhancing confidence-building measures and technical assistance to implement and administer export control regulations. In July 2005, India and the US signed a deal leading to civilian nuclear cooperation and though, some members of the EU opposed the deal, France whole-heartedly supported India and often reiterated its readiness to supply nuclear technology, especially to sell advanced nuclear reactors so as help India in meeting out its energy requirements. The American, Russian and French corporations in the nuclear field started negotiations with India in right earnestness and already a couple of agreements have been signed in this regard. It is significant to note that the nuclear apartheid with regard to India came to an end when it signed its commercial nuclear deal with the French nuclear giant Areva for nuclear reactors and fuel supply in February 2009. [26]

There is notable convergence of opinion between India and the EU that NPT should be non-discriminatory in character and both the parties believe that indefinite extension of the status quo or an uncertain foray into unilateral disarmament is unworkable. Both the powers are conscious of the need for coordinated efforts at joint reduction and eventual elimination of nuclear weapons and on the need to prevent nuclear weapons from falling into wrong hands. The Joint Statement issued at the November 2007 India-EU Summit said that the partners "would preserve and promote peaceful uses of technology through forward looking approaches among countries committed to disarmament and non-proliferation", and this statement is considered by Radha Kumar implying EU's attempt to coyly accepting the India-US civilian nuclear energy cooperation agreement. [27] However, the lack of a cohesive EU approach is compounded by the fact that it is individual states, and not the EU, which are signatories to the NPT regime and in the position to acknowledge the need for a differentiated approach. [28]

Known convergences and divergences apart, it seems that the EU is not serious in restricting India's ambition on the nuclear front. Though the European Commission passed a resolution expecting India to sign NPT and CTBT in June 2002, in October 2002, it was silent on the issue. [29] Again, the EU usually introduced a conditionality clause to its trade agreements requiring treaty partners to effectively support non-proliferation at their domestic level. In case of important trading partners like India, such clauses have not been introduced and implemented with sincerity. [30] One more fact that calls for attention is that in the wake of India-US civilian nuclear cooperation, the EU endorsed India's participation in the International Thermonuclear Experimental Reactor (ITER) project, thereby doing amends to its inability to do what the US was capable of. India joining the ITER project, a unique international futuristic endeavour with a strong European dimension, has emblematic value for India's status. [31]

The Europeans continue to help the Indian Government to achieve Millennium Development Goals (MDGs) such as poverty eradication, education etc. through its development assistance. At the India-EU Summit at New Delhi on September 7, 2005, a Joint Action Plan (JAP) was adopted as an evolving roadmap outlining concrete actions to operationalise the partnership. Again, a memorandum of understanding was signed on the Country Strategy Paper for India 2007-2010.

The Union pledged to offer € 260 million, around 60 percent of available funds to meeting the MDGs, which signals the strong commitment of the EU to India overcoming the challenge of poverty and its achieving its MDGs in a time bound way. [32] The rest was allocated to implement the JAP. The JAP also maps out cooperation on a wide range of subjects, some of which are quite substantive: India has joined the Galileo satellite navigation project; the EU is backing Indian participation in the ITER nuclear fusion reactor; Indian researchers take part in the EU's R&D programmes; many hundreds of Indian students receive Erasmus Mundus scholarships; and a new 'joint initiative on clean development and climate change' involves the EU funding the diffusion of green technologies in India. [33]

Subsequently, the Plan was reviewed in 2008 Summit in Marseilles and was expanded to include diverse areas for action.

As such, the JAP between the two parties proves to be of great importance and relevance. Subsequently, the EU Country Strategy Paper for India (2007-2013) was brought out. The strategy set out in this paper consists of two pillars. [34] While the first forms the basis of the EU's future development cooperation so that India is able to achieve the MDGs by 2015, the second pillar concerns with the implementation of JAP. [35]

To put it in a nutshell, it may be concluded that the EU recognises India as a major power and an influential global actor and expects emerging India to take international responsibilities commensurate with its international aspirations and status and offers its cooperation and assistance in this regard. Mandelson was forthright when he pronounced in his 2005 address in Kolkata, "I look to India to assume the risks and responsibilities of leadership, and I offer you Europe's partnership in doing so". [36]

Section IV

In spite of all these positive developments, some scholars, both European and Indian, argue that the EU-India strategic partnership, which was launched more than a decade ago, is yet to take off. It is considered to be ineffective and has failed to deliver the desired output and to achieve something substantial, in spite of the potential behind the two powers as well as the better prospects that the partnership enjoy. Its positive contributions are being neglected and ignored by both the Indian and the European scholars.

While Gauri Khandekar considers that India-EU strategic partnership is one of the most static and disappointing of such accords and likens it to 'loveless arranged marriage' between a well-matched couple but with no spark of chemistry, [37] Christophe Jaffrelot terms the India-EU strategic partnership as the charade, pretense, and sham. [38]

A study titled, "Evaluating India's Strategic Partnerships using Analytic Hierarchy Process" conducted by Sarita Azad and Arvind Gupta and published by the Institute of Defence

Studies and Analyses, a leading think-tank from New Delhi, in September 2011, just like that, ignores India's strategic partnership with the EU. [39] Yet another study titled, "India's Strategic Partners: A Comparative Assessment", conducted by a group of foreign policy and strategic analysts associated with the Foundation for National Security Research (FNSR), New Delhi, in November 2011, too assessed India's strategic partnerships, and has sought to identify what India should seek from these partnerships. It has weighed India's strategic partnership with six countries—United States, Russia, France, United Kingdom, Germany, and Japan—by grading them on a 10-point scale for present performance, sustainability, and potential of these partnerships for India in three areas of co-operation: political-diplomatic ties; defence ties; and economic relations.

The Report is categorical while maintaining that the Indian strategic partnership with Russia is more effective than the ones with the US, Japan and the member states of the EU. FNSR has conveniently ignored the India-EU partnership without even referring to it, as if of no consequence. The Report concludes that India should not bestow the "respectable nomenclature" of a strategic partner on one and all, but only on those countries with which there is "a strong and mutually beneficial relationship" in all three sectors—political-diplomatic; defence and economic co-operation and suggests that for its so-called strategic agreements with a host of other countries, such as the one with the EU, India needs to find a "less serious" nomenclature. [40]

Section V

Several factors caused such a setback and the main being reluctance on the part of the two powers to believe and behave as security and strategic actors at the global level. Generally, it is believed that India lacks strategic culture, while some scholars maintain that the Indians possessed certain strategic culture ever since the ancient times and refer to *Arthsastra* of

Chanakya. While maintaining that India-EU strategic partnership currently lacks substance and strategic weight and Europe and India have divergent approaches to addressing security issues, Shashi Tharoor is candid that India has not yet evolved a comprehensive national security strategy to cover the entire spectrum of threats that it faces. He further argues that even if Europe desires closer security cooperation with India as of now, the latter is in no position to reciprocate except in terms of generalities. Again, Tharoor is categorical when he says that as a democracy, India needs to undertake a strategic defence review that covers all elements of the security services, elected representatives in Parliament, the public at large and to produce a national security strategy. His remorse is that such an exercise has not even been contemplated and attempted so far. [41]

It is heartening to note that the first step towards the right direction has been taken in 2012 by the articulation of the policy paper titled, "Nonalignment 2.0: A Foreign and Strategic Policy for India in the Twenty-first Century", authored by a group of leading thinkers, scholars, former diplomats and soldiers, and public figures including Sunil Khilnani, Rajiv Kumar, Pratap Bhanu Mehta, Lt. Gen. (Retd.) Prakash Menon, Nandan Nilekani, Srinath Raghavan, Shyam Saran and Siddharth Varadarajan, which expectedly provoked an informative national debate and initiated the exercise towards consensus-building in the Indian foreign and strategic policy formulation and execution. [42]

Again, India is at times rated as a soft state, which is not in a position to safeguard its borders from incursions of the terrorist groups and to properly protect the national interest. Even the Indian opposition leaders, in their interest to denigrate the government of the day, indulge in this sort of propaganda, thereby bringing down the image of the country and the morale of the security forces guarding the border. While analyzing four of the deficits of India's foreign-military policy, Bharat Karnad maintains that lack of strategy remains one of them, besides vision, conviction and will. [43]

C. Raja Mohan, well-known Indian strategic analyst captures India's foreign policy stance by the image of the porcupine—'vegetarian, slow-footed and prickly' and maintains that defensiveness usually remained "the hallmark of Indian approach to the world". He further adds that as a reactive power, India put up its sharp quills to ward off the threats, when the world impinges on it. [44] Further building on this depiction of India, Mark Leonard, Director of the Foreign Policy Centre, London, maintains that this image perception hints at the perceived vulnerability of New Delhi's international agency, which 'uses its quills to deter aggressors and hides in a cave, especially when Pakistan is mentioned'. [45] Pakistani mischief and international community's compliance with it forces India to withdraw itself from any unsavoury environment.

On the other hand, even a casual observer notices certain reluctance on the part of the EC/EU to speak on defence and security matters ever since the failure of the attempt to establish a European Defence Community. Only in the 1990s, the Europeans could overcome this reluctance. Most probably due to the fact that the strategic partnerships inevitably cover two dimensions—a strategic approach to foreign policy and in developing bilateral relations with third powers in which the Union has traditionally been quite ineffective, the EU belatedly forging them. [46]

Although all EU member states have always attended to military planning and procurement, both individually and collectively in association with organizations such as the North Atlantic Treaty Organisation (NATO) and the Western European Union (WEU), discussion of such matters within the confines of the EU was always regarded as taboo and the Union continued too set its face against discussion on security and defence issues. Member states like the UK too were, and continue to be, against any meaningful discussion on security and defence matters at the Union level. It was in no way less due to the parallel existence of the WEU, a body whose sole *raison d'être* was to coordinate the European thinking of its member states in the field of security and defence policy and to render this compatible with the NATO. [47]

Though there was an attempt to draft a strategic doctrine in the 1990s under the auspices of the WEU, the European Security Strategy of 2003 was the first ever strategic doctrine that came out from the Union.

As in the case of India, the EU too is considered and scornfully referred to as an economic giant, military worm and a political pigmy. Its 'civilian' and 'soft' power posture is taken as its weakness. Its preference for multilateralism with the UN at its centre and option for negotiation as a tool to sort out problems, is attributed to its lack of capacity to force its point of view on others. Robert Kagan has contemptuously framed the international identity of the EU through the figure of Venus and hence, in contrast to the might of the American Mars, Brussels' alleged effete civilian power lacks the capabilities to deter non-compliance and to punish disobedience. [48]

It is rather ironic that the well-conceived and more sensible civilian approach of the EU as well as the restraint practiced by India in the face of Pakistani affront is considered as weakness by the other partners as well as by the international community, which respects and recognizes power politics, hard power potentials rather than civilian, and soft power approach. Resulting catastrophes in the international politics demand change in the mindset that respects goodness for its own sake.

Though India and the EU are strategic actors of limited extent and means, both think that the other is strategic partner in a limited sense. While the Indians feel that the EU as such is not yet ripe to act as a credible political partner, the European view tends to be that "India is either not ready to take on the responsibilities commensurate with its growing ambitions or is in fact buying time so as to defer acting as a responsible actor in the international arena". [49] This problem of mutual indifference has become a vicious circle. While the strategic relations with the other strategic partners of the EU such as China are better developed and are therefore attracting more attention from the Union, on the other hand, relations with India is not a priority, and as such remains less developed, resulting in India's status as the weakest strategic partner of the EU.

Despite vast potentials, the strategic partnership between the EU and India does not seem to be either's absolute priority. The Indian security perspectives are much closer to the US than the EU model. As a consequence, the US model for security in Asia is taken much more seriously by Asian powers and the US figures much more prominently in India's foreign policy considerations. The European emphasis on multilateralism and supranational institutions are diametrically opposed to India's adherence to bilateralism and the principle of sovereignty as in the case of the US strategic thinking. As a result, India is much more comfortable in its security dealings with the US and even individual EU member states than with the EU. [50]

Lack of understanding and appreciation on the part of the Europeans regarding India's security concerns in an unstable and invariably hostile neighbourhood remains a constant irritant for the Indians. The South Asian security environment has prompted a greater focus on military dimensions and on hard power capabilities. [51] India feels that the EU is of no consequence in its dealings with the South Asian neighbours.

While India is currently focusing on the United States, especially as a hedge against the growth of Chinese power, the EU's Sino-centrism make it hardly figuring on the Indian radar screen. [52] Fraser Cameron too concurs with this view and maintains that for Indians, the EU does not appear on their radar screens as a political and security actor. [53]

Most Indian policy makers and analysts are still sceptical about the EU's role as a major strategic player in Asia, with the result that it is hardly a factor in India's current foreign policy debates. Moreover, 'Europe is often conspicuously absent in important discussions of Indian grand strategy'. [54] From India's perspective, the EU has potential to play an important role—economically and politically, if not militarily—in New Delhi's realist approach to achieving security characterized by efforts aimed at "managing asymmetries, not eliminating them, [and managing] the multi-cornered strategic context to India's advantage". [55]

Brussels has been unable to articulate what role it sees for India in the emerging security architecture. [56] Bernd von Muenchow-Pohl argues that 'there is only partial overlap between what each side hopes to get out of the partnership'. Both, he says, '[s]hare common objectives, but these relate more to general principles for the global order than to details and deliverables'. [57] Similarly, C. Raja Mohan had argued that 'India's relations with Europe have been limited by the fact that New Delhi is fairly unimpressed with Europe's role in global politics'. [58]

Karine Lisbonne-de-Vergeron, who has studied contemporary Indian views of Europe, points out that Europe has failed to express any strategic political vision, especially in military terms; its own divisions further push towards favouring bilateral relationships and India's leading strategic interests are not currently converging towards those of Europe. [59] The last factor comes out very clearly, while assessing the way in which both the strategic partners work within the UN System, The fact that India voted against the EU almost every other time during the 2004-2009, suggests a diverging view between the two partners on world affairs. [60] It is noteworthy that the voting cohesion significantly drops to levels of around 50 percent or even less on development and human rights issues.

Strategic partners like India, prefer to work with nation-states instead of the supranational EU, which is increasingly regarded by them as a "trend". [61] Individual member states have a considerable military presence in the region and maintain military dialogues, joint exercises, arms sales, technology transfers, and so on. With their preference for bilateralism in security matters, India continues to deal with the individual member states. [62] EU appears to be playing a diminishing role in India's strategic thinking, despite its strong relations with the individual member countries of the Union such as Britain, France and Germany. Indians generally believe that the EU provides relatively little added value to major security challenges faced by them relating to China, South and Central Asia and the Middle East. [63] Unless the EU adds value in its dealings with India than the good relations traditionally enjoyed by the latter with its member states, the Union cannot impress on India to deal with it directly.

Differentiation on the perception of strategic partnership and what is to be achieved by such an arrangement too remain yet another factor. There is no common understanding between the parties on what role the strategic partnership should play in achieving their foreign and strategic policy goals. India envisaged a relationship of sovereign equality based on comparative advantage and a mutuality of interests and benefits and for the Indians the strategic partnership is about recognizing potential and about engaging each other on a varied range of issues. To the Europeans, a strategic partnership implies a global economic and political relationship involving the sharing of global responsibility and the building of a "coalition of interests" to meet the challenges of the twenty-first century, whereas for India, a strategic partnership with the EU complements its efforts to emerge as a major power in world politics. These differences in perceptions on the very purpose of strategic partnership, makes the formulation and realization of any meaningful common interests.

EU's normative approaches in distant regions, such as attempts to pledge India to various international standards, whether it is environmental standards or human rights, are slowing down the process and purpose of dialogue. [64] The Union's post-modern pretensions and advocacy of civilian or soft power approach to India, without botheration to the fact that the latter is situated in a region where the defence of national sovereignty might be crucial for the cohesion of the state, makes India feel that the EU is of no consequence as a security partner. No wonder that a cable released in early 2011 by WikiLeaks quotes an Indian official saying that the EU is too "obvious, shabby, short-sighted, full of contradictions, naïve, overly pro-active, and possessing a tendency to go overboard when it comes to delicate issues". [65] The Europeans should recognize the fact that the partnership will be driven by mutual interests rather than mutual values.

Renard maintains that a closer look at the substance of the partnerships concluded by the EU with other partners in general and with India in particular, "clearly reveals their lack of strategic character". [66] Strategy is missing in the India-EU partnership. Strategic partnerships are commonly associated with defence or security related issues, but the India-EU strategic partnership has become quite a hold-all, covering a wide range in bilateral relations, from defence to education, health and agriculture, and quite prominently, economic relations including trade, investment and banking. [67] The European leaders give more prominence to trade enhancement and market opening than to security, in this partnership. On the two strategic questions that matter most to India—its putative deal with the US to end its nuclear isolation, and its bid for a permanent seat in the UN Security Council—the EU has proved incapable of forging a common position and be of any meaningful help to India. [68]

Section VI

These factors which cause the ineffectiveness and under-delivery of the strategic partnership between India and the EU makes one wonder whether India-EU Strategic Partnership, is a failure. It is already noticed that on several spheres, India-EU partnership has delivered substantially, especially for India. The study titled "India's Strategic Partners: A Comparative

Assessment", of which reference has been made earlier, has assessed India's strategic partnerships by grading them on a 10-point scale for present performance, sustainability, and potential of these partnerships for India in three areas of co-operation: political-diplomatic ties; defence ties; and economic relations. In one of the areas of cooperation—economic relations—India-EU partnership remains solid and sound. The EU is the largest trade partner of India with bilateral trade amounting to US$ 126 billion a year and also the largest export destination for India and a source of US$ 68 billion in FDI. Mention has already been made about the EU's role in India for achieving the targets of MDGs by 2015. As such, under these criteria, the India-EU strategic partnership is undoubtedly effective and has delivered impressive results.

In the sphere of political and diplomatic ties, India-EU partnership helped India in boosting its image. The India-EU Strategic Partnership is a qualitative transformation in the way the parties engage as equal partners and work together in partnership with the world at large. In the field of civilian nuclear cooperation and on the question of Indian claim for UNSC permanent membership, the partnership may not be effective. EU's support in the latter case is of no value and is therefore immaterial. Success and effectiveness of the India-EU strategic partnership need not be and should not be tied down to the failure of the Union on this count. On the same count, India's unwillingness to finalise and sign the FTA with the EU, which pending even since the negotiations started in 2007, too need not be linked to it.

Defence ties between the partners, especially in the traditional sense, may be weak. However, on meeting out the non-traditional security threats, the India-EU partnership can even be more effective. India needs help and partnership from the EU in facing and tackling NTS threats, especially in its poverty eradication programme and in this regard, the EU may be of great help.

Section VII

Now, the inevitable question, how to make the Partnership further effective, begs an answer. India and the EU should shed their ambiguity and reservations and should further strategize the strategic partnership between them so as to achieve its objectives. They should develop into fully-fledged global security and strategic actors and work towards facing the traditional and as well as non-traditional security threats squarely. Sebastian Kastner feels that the India-EU partnership is "beneath potentials" and is categorical in pointing out that "the need for success remains that of mutual respect and trust building". [69] Luis Peral maintains that neither India nor the EU seem to be "fully-fledged 'strategic' international actors themselves; but they may well at some point realise that they need to work more closely together so as to address their respective internal problems more effectively, even if it entails redefining themselves as genuine strategic actors". [70]

Some others believe that both the parties do not have any common strategic interest and such a point of view is far from reality. The EU and India do have shared strategic interests to face common security threats and challenges, stemming in from the zones of instability that lie between them and any escalation of tension in the Middle East or Central Asia could threaten EU-India trade, compromise their energy security and result in terrorist attacks. The probability of such risks is high and real, and this factor may push the EU into a real strategic dialogue with India in the near future. [71] Both the parties need to keep the institutionalized, structured strategic dialogue mechanism ready for such an eventuality as and when it arises.

Coulon also adverts that to facilitate a fruitful cooperation on global security issues "it is essential that the EU hears India's security concerns and adapts its dialogue accordingly, even if it involves putting aside references to moral values and international norms in trying to answer India's most urgent security concerns". [72]

From the European side, there is a lingering grouse that the initiative to develop the strategic partnership predominantly comes from their side and an expectation that more Indian engagement would be highly desirable. Both the parties need to take the other's point of view more seriously, so as to make the partnership more effective and deliverable. The need of the hour is that both the parties should try to finalise agreements on maritime security, nuclear security and other such cooperative and collaborative mechanisms so that the partnership will be more in practice than on paper alone. The partnership should become more action oriented than mere rhetoric, hollow statements and wish list. No wonder that Abhyankar rates the partnership between India and the EU as the one for 'all reasons'. [73] It is for 'all seasons' as well.

Endnotes

1. Christopher Hill, "The Capability-Expectations Gap, or Conceptualizing Europe's International Role", *Journal of Common Market Studies,* Vol. 31, No. 3, September 1993, p. 324. EU's external relations is regulated by the concept of 'concentric circles' or the notion of the 'pyramid of privileges', whereby states like the US form the closest ring around the EU, followed by a belt including the CSCE, ASEAN, China, Japan and India, and then, another constituted by the African, Caribbean and Pacific and Asian and Latin American countries. The EU's relations with these countries vary in warmth and intensity and while with some it is simple exchange relationship, in the case of some others, economic assistance and incentives are involved aiming at long-term patterns of friendship and stability. As of now, the EU has strategic partnership with the US, Russia, Canada, Japan, China and India, which makes the relationship maintained by the Union with these countries something 'special', more intensive and rigorous.
2. 'A Secure Europe in a Better World: European Security Strategy', Brussels: EUISS and European Commission, December 12, 2003, (henceforth ESS), available at: http://www.consilium.europa.eu/uedocs/cmsUpload/78367.pdf.
3. Christian Wagner, "The EU and India: A Deepening Partnership". Giovanni Grevi and Alvaro de Vasconcelos (eds.), 'Partnerships for Effective Multilateralism: EU Relations with

Brazil, China, India and Russia", Chaillot Paper, No. 109, European Union Institute for Security Studies, Paris, May 2008, p. 87.

4. "An EU-India Strategic Partnership", Brussels: European Commission [COM (2004) 430 final], pp. 7, 9, June 16, available at: http://eurlex.europa.eu/LexUriServ/LexUriServ.do?uri=COM:2004:0430:FIN:EN:PDF.
5. Fifth India-EU Summit, The Hague, November 8, 2004, Joint Press Statement.
6. Political Declaration on the India-EU Strategic Partnership, Brussels, September 7, 2005, 11985/05 (Presse 224).
7. R.K. Jain, "India-EU Strategic Partnership: Perceptions and Perspectives", NFG Working Paper No. 10, July 2014, p. 7.
8. Paul M. Kennedy (ed.), "Grand Strategies in War and Peace", (New Haven: Yale University Press, 1991), p. 5.
9. R.K. Jain, n. 7, p. 7.
10. Thomas Renard, "The EU Strategic Partnerships Review: Ten Guiding Principles", ESPO, Policy Brief 2, April 2012, p. 4.
11. ESS, pp. 14, 33.
12. Thomas Renard and Sven Biscop, "Conclusion: From Global Disorder to an Effective Multilateral Order: An Agenda for the EU", pp. 185-198, at pp. 196-197, in Thomas Renard and Sven Biscop (eds.) 'The European Union and Emerging Powers in the 21st Century: How Europe Can Shape a New Global Order', Farnham, Surrey: Ashgate, 2012.
13. Natalie M. Hess, "EU Relations with 'Emerging' Strategic Partners: Brazil, India and South Africa", GIGA Focus No. 4, 2012, p. 2.
14. Thomas Renard, "The Treachery of Strategies: A Call for True EU Strategic Partnerships", Egmont Paper 45, April 2011, p. 6.
15. European Commission, "Trade, Growth and World Affairs: Trade Policy as a Core Component of the EU's 2020 Strategy 2010", p. 12, available at: http://eur-lex.europa.eu/legal-content/EN/TXT/PDF/?uri=CELEX:52010DC0612&from=EN.
16. Anne Coulon, "EU-India Understandings on Major Global Political Issues: Where do We Stand"?, p. 340, available at: www.jnu.ac.in.
17. Renard, n. 14, p. 23.

18. Catherine Ashton, (2012), "Speech on EU Foreign Policy towards the BRICS and other Emerging Powers (SPEECH/12/56)", available at: http://eeas.europa.eu/ images/top stories/020212_brics.pdf.
19. "Kashmir Integral Part of India: EU", available at: http://www.defence.pk/forums/world-affairs/39879-j-k-integral-part-india-eu-delegation.html.
20. "EU Report on Kashmir Criticises Pakistan", available at: http://www.rediff.com/news/2007/may/25eupak.htm. The report was passed by an overwhelming majority with 522 votes in its favour and nine against it.
21. European Parliament committee adopts pro-India Kashmir report, *Malaysia Sun*, March 21, 2007, available at: http://www.charlestannock.com/pressarticle.asp?ID=1560.
22. Bennett-Jones Owen (2007), "Musharraf's Kashmir Policy", *Asian Affairs*, Vol. 38, No. 3, pp. 315-316.
23. J.N. Dixit (1996), "My South Block Years: Memoirs of a Foreign Secretary", UBS Publishers' Distributors Ltd., New Delhi, p. 276.
24. Karen E. Smith (2008), "European Union Foreign Policy in a Changing World Polity", Cambridge, Second Edition, p. 61.
25. B. Krishnamurthy (2005), "Indo-French Relations: Problems and Perspectives", Shipra Publications, New Delhi. Refer Chapter 9 on Indo-French nuclear cooperation.
26. *The Hindu* (Chennai), February 5, 2009.
27. Radha Kumar, "India as a Foreign Policy Actor: Normative Redux", CEPS Working Document No. 285/February 2008, p. 23, available at: http://www.ceps.eu.
28. Ummu Salma Bava (2008), "The EU and India: Challenges to a Strategic Partnership", Giovanni and Alvaro de Vasconcelos (eds.), 'Partnerships for Effective Multilateralism: EU Relations with Brazil, China, India and Russia', Chaillot Paper, No. 109, May, p. 107.
29. Jean-Luc Racine (2004), "European Union and South Asia: An Appraisal" in 'Major Powers in South Asia', Institute of Regional Studies, Islamabad, pp. 131-162. Racine raises an interesting issue: "One wonders what expectations were behind such a rhetorical statement. That the joint press statement issued at the end of the third EU-India Summit, in October 2002, said

nothing about nuclear issues, answers perhaps this question".

30. Christian Mölling (2010), "The Grant Bargain in the NPT: Challenges for the EU beyond 2010", in Ian Anthony, Camille Grand, Łukasz Kulesa, Christian Mölling, Mark Smith, 'Nuclear Weapons after the 2010 NPT Review Conference', (ed.) Jean Pascal Zanders, Chaillot Papers 120, Institute for Security Studies, European Union, Paris, April, p. 59.
31. Jean Luc-Racine (2007), "The India-Europe Relationship in the US Shadow", Rajendra K. Jain, 'India and the European Union: Building a Strategic Partnership', Radiant Publishers, New Delhi, pp. 59-60. India and the EU have signed several bilateral agreements, which include one providing for cooperation in the field of Science and Technology in 2001. In a programme under this framework, India joined in December 2005 with six other countries—the EU, Japan, the US, Russia, China and South Korea—for launching the ITER to be built up in France.
32. Wagner, n. 3, p. 102.
33. Charles Grant, "India and the EU: Strategic Partners"?, Centre for European Reform, February/March 2006, CER Bulletin, Issue 46, available at: http://www.cer.org.uk/articles/46_grant.html.
34. European Commission, "India: Country Strategy Paper 2007-2013", available at: http://www.eeas.europa.eu/india/csp/07_13_en.pdf.
35. Wagner, n. 3, pp. 87-88.
36. Peter Mandelson, speech, "The Global Economic Agenda: Europe and India's Challenge", Confederation of Indian Industry Partnership Summit, Kolkata, January 13, 2005.
37. Gauri Khandekar, "The EU and India: A Loveless Arranged Marriage", FRIDE Policy Brief No. 90, August 2011.
38. Christophe Jaffrelot, "India and the European Union: The Charade of the Strategic Partnership", *Eurasia Bulletin,* Vol. 10, #1&2, January-February 2006, pp. 4-6.
39. Sarita Azad and Arvind Gupta (2011), "Evaluating India's Strategic Partnerships using Analytic Hierarchy Process", Institute of Defence Studies and Analyses, New Delhi, September.
40. Foundation for National Security Research, "India's Strategic Partners: A Comparative Assessment", New Delhi, November 2011.

41. Shashi Tharoor (2012), "PaxIndica: India and the World of the 21st Century", Penguin Books, New Delhi, pp. 245, 412.
42. Sunil Khilnani et al. (2012), "Non-alignment 2.0.: A Foreign and Strategic Policy for India in the Twenty-First Century", Centre for Policy Research, New Delhi.
43. Bharat Karnad (2006), "Vision, Conviction, Strategy, and Will: The Four Deficits in India's Foreign-Military Policy", in M. Malhoutra (ed.), 'India: The Next Decade', Academic Foundation, New Delhi, p. 494.
44. C. Raja Mohan (2004), "Crossing the Rubicon: The Shaping of India's New Foreign Policy", London, Palgrave, p. 260.
45. Mark Leonard, "India Joins the West", *Prospect*, November 15, 2005, p. 10, available at: http://www.cer.org.uk/articles/leonard_prospect_november05.html.
46. Renard, n. 14, p. 1.
47. Jolyon Howorth, "Saint-Malo Plus Five: An Interim Assessment of ESDP", p. 3, available at: http://www.institutdelors.eu/media/policypaper7.pdf?pdf=ok.
48. Robert Kagan (2003), "Of Paradise and Power: America and Europe in the New World Order", New York, NY: Knopf.
49. Álvaro de Vasconcelos (ed.) (2010), "A Strategy for EU Foreign Policy", Report N° 7, June, p. 72.
50. NFG Conference Report, "Europe's Role for Security in a Multipolar World: Views from India and China", New Delhi, 26th-27th September, 2013, p. 13.
51. Florian Britsch (2014), "Indian Views of Europe's Role as Security Actor: Why the EU Needs to Change its Approach towards India", April, p. 1.
52. Rajendra M. Abhyankar, "India and the European Union: Non-associable to Strategic Partner", in Atish Sinha and Madhup Mohta (eds.), 'Indian Foreign Policy: Challenges and Opportunities' New Delhi: Academic Foundation, 2007, pp. 449-466, at p. 464.
53. Fraser Cameron, "India and the EU: A Long Road Ahead", in Harsha V. Pant (ed.) 'Indian Foreign Policy in a Unipolar World', Routledge India, New Delhi, 2009, p. 223.
54. D. Jaishankar, "Europe in Indian Strategy" in K. Venkatshamy and P. George (eds.), 'Grand Strategy for India 2020 and Beyond', New Delhi: Institute for Defence Studies and

Analyses, Pentagon Security International, 2012, p. 242.

55. A. Kapur (2006), "India: From Regional to World Power", Oxon: Routledge, p. 43.
56. Harsh V. Pant, "After Word", in Pant, n. 53, p. 329.
57. B. von Muenchow-Pohl (2012), "India and Europe in a Multi Polar World", Washington DC: Carnegie Endowment for International Peace, pp. 1-2.
58. C. Raja Mohan, "India and the Balance of Power", *Foreign Affairs*, July-August, 2006.
59. KarineLisbonne-de-Vergeron (2006), "Contemporary Indian Views of Europe", Chatham House, London, p. 7.
60. Thomas Renard and Bas Hooijmaaijers, "Assessing the EU's Strategic Partnerships in the UN System", p. 1, *Egmont Security Policy Brief*, No. 23, May 2011.
61. Hess, n. 13, p. 6.
62. NFG Report, n. 50, pp. 9, 11.
63. Gulshan Sachdeva, "Evaluation of the EU-India Strategic Partnership and the Potential for its Revitalization", p. 10, available at: http://www.europarl.europa.eu/RegData/etudes/STUD/2015/534987/EXPO_STU% 282015%29534987_EN.pdf.
64. Sebastian Kastner, "Beneath Potentials? EU-India Relations", p. 47, available at: http://lup.lub.lu.se/luur/download?func=downloadFile&recordOId=1320265&fileOId=1320266.
65. http://www.thehindu.com/news/the-india-cables/thecables/article1554270.ece.
66. Renard, n. 14, p. 5.
67. Nirupama Subramanian, "In the Promiscuous World of International Relations, Elements of a Strategic Partnership", available at: http://www.thehindu.com/opinion/op-ed/in-the-promiscuous-world-of-international-relations-elements-of-a-strategic-partnership/article2806158.ece.
68. Charles Grant, "How the Rising Powers View the EU", *Issues*, November 2007, Newsletter of the EU Institute of Security Studies, available at: www.iss.europa.eu.
69. Kastner, n. 64, p. 48.
70. Luis Peral, "Introduction: Setting the EU-India Partnership in

Motion" in Luis Peral and Vijay Sakhuja, 'The EU-India Partnership: Time to go Strategic"?, The EU Institute for Security Studies, Paris, 2012, p. 12.

71. Richard Gowanand and Sushant K. Singh, "Atlas of Indo-European Strategy", December 19 2010, available at: http://www.livemint.com/Opinion/Q5YFMHRkr4SIWefdM5D48J/Atlas-of-IndoEuropean-strategy.html.
72. Coulon, n. 16, p. 348.
73. Rajendra M. Abhyankar, "India and the European Union: A Partnership for All Reasons", *India Quarterly*, Vol. 65, No. 4, 2009, pp. 393-404.

8

India's Climate Change Policy: Paris Conference and Beyond

Anu Unny

Climate change issue has emerged as a major issue of concern in international politics since 1970s. Today, it has become 'the defining challenge of our age' (KI-Moon, 2007). The fourth and fifth assessment reports of the Intergovernmental Panel on Climate Change (IPCC) warn that India will be among the countries that are likely to be worst affected by climate change. The devastating effects of climate change has already started to destabilise the livelihood of the people leading to steep fall in agriculture production, submergence of coastal areas and extreme events such as floods and cyclones. Though these effects are transnational, still there is lack of consensus among major state actors especially among India, China and the United States over how to address this climate crisis.

Even in the Warsaw Conference concluded in 2013 and in the Lima Climate Change Conference in 2014, major developed and developing countries were busily engaging in hard bargaining in pursuit of their narrow self-interests rather than addressing this larger problem collectively. It was in order to break this deadlock, that the world nations met at Paris in December 2015 with the objective to give form to a new international agreement that can replace the Kyoto Protocol. The Paris agreement which was given form after a lot of discussions and deliberations finally adopted a bottom to top approach marking a departure from the Kyoto styled top to bottom approach in emission reduction.

Before the beginning of the Paris Conference, almost all major polluting countries had submitted their Intended Nationally Determined Contributions (hereafter INDCs) to the United Nations Framework Convention on Climate Change (hereafter UNFCCC) based on their national circumstances and capabilities. India's 38 page INDC document submitted to the UNFCCC clearly states that India would strive to reduce the emission intensity of its GDP from 33 to 35 percent from 2005 level by 2030. Secondly, India's INDC document promises that India would try to produce at least 40 percent of its cumulative electric power capacity from energy sources that are non-fossil fuel ones.

Thirdly, India would give form to a carbon sink of 2.5 billion to 3 billion tonnes of CO_2 equivalent by expanding its forest cover by 2030 (Government of India, 2015). The central question is whether India would be able to fulfil its INDC target by 2030 especially in the context of its growing emissions. While examining this, this paper also makes an attempt to trace the climate change policy of India till date.

Evolution of India's Climate Change Policy

While tracing the evolution of India's climate change policy, the 1972 Stockholm Conference was significant as it was the first major conference India participated actively engaging with the environmental issues at the international level. However, at Stockholm, Prime Minister Indira Gandhi had to make it clear that 'for the country, eradicating poverty is the top most priority at that stage than all other environmental considerations'. She unequivocally stated that "for India, poverty is the greatest polluter and development is the healer" (June 14, 1972).

Consequently, poverty reduction and achieving better economic growth dominated the Indian environmental thinking in its first phase. In the second phase of the environmentalism which began in 1980s, major focus was on how to strike a balance between the environmental and developmental concerns. India could project itself as a champion of 'sustainable development' at this stage by acknowledging and accepting the recommendations of Brundtland Commission which floated the idea that development must be holistic and longstanding. The Brundtland report placed environmental issues firmly on the political agenda in the search for a sustainable development path. The Report treated environment and development as one single issue area and defined the concept of 'sustainable development' as the "development that meets the needs of the present without compromising the ability of the future generations to meet their own needs" (World Commission on Environment and Development, 1987).

The third phase of Indian environmentalism and climate change campaign started in 1990s. The depletion of ozone layer, acid rain, increasing pollution and changing climate pattern accelerated the efforts of the environmentalists to give form to a climate change regime. In the 1992 Rio Conference, for the first time, countries came together with a resolve to fight against global warming. The Rio Summit provided the basic architectures (political, legal and normative structures) to deal with the climate change challenge. From the very beginning of Rio negotiations, India had upheld the motto of 'sustainable development' and 'equity'.

With the 1991 economic crisis and with the emergence of a new U.S. dominated world system at the end of Cold War, it was quite rational for India to build its arguments based on the principles of equity and justice. In the Conference, India argued that those, countries namely developed countries, which have polluted the atmosphere must take up more emission reduction responsibilities than developing countries that have polluted less. India was advocating passionately for a common but differentiated approach towards developing countries at the Rio Conference. The Kyoto Protocol, the first legally binding emission reduction agreement that came into form in 1997 was based on this principle of Common but Differentiated Responsibility (hereafter CBDR).

If one examines India's climate change policy, it can be easily understood that throughout all these years, climate policy of the country was dependent upon three principles—responsibility, right and capacity. Responsibility factor upholds the 'polluter pays' principle. It maintains that, those countries that have polluted the atmosphere must bear the brunt of emissions (here developed countries). 'Right' refers to the right to have equal per capita emissions. It indicates that each and every individual on this earth has equal right to a minimum of socio-economic welfare. Hence, each individual must be able to enjoy the same per capita emission right as any other individual in a developed country enjoys. Capacity denotes to the 'ability to pay'. It refers to the fact that socio-economic circumstances of the countries are different. Hence, it is the moral responsibility of rich industrialized countries to support developing countries technologically and financially to fight against the odds of climate change.

At the Cancun Conference in 2010, world nations had given form to a 'Green Climate Fund' to assist developing countries in the mobilization of resources. Nevertheless, as of December 2014, developing countries have received only a fraction of the amount pledged by the developed world. During the recent visit of Prime Minister Modi to China, both the countries had brought out a statement demanding developed countries to fulfil their promises made in that respect.

The 2009 Copenhagen Conference marked a shift in India's long standing position on climate change. This can be labelled as the beginning of the fourth phase of Indian environmentalism. For the first time in the Conference deliberations, the then Minister for Environment and Forest Jairam Ramesh stated that 'India must go beyond the traditional per capita approach to a per capita plus approach considering India's rising global status as the leader of the developing world' (Sarkar, 2009). In the 2010 Cancun Conference, Ramesh stated that "all countries must take up binding emission reduction commitments under appropriate legal platform" (PTI, 2010). Though Minister Jairam Ramesh had to go back from this statement later on in the Parliament, in redefining and giving an entirely new orientation and dimension to India's climate change policy, Jairam Ramesh's contributions were remarkable.

India's INDC submission to the UNFCCC on October 2, 2015 can be seen as another turning point in India's climate change campaign at the international level. India's INDC document submitted to the UNFCCC clearly states that it would reduce its level of emissions drastically by 2030. Though India has already made it clear that fulfilment of India's INDC target is partially dependent upon the transfer of financial and technological resources from developed countries to it, India's ambitious emission reduction plan is a hint that the country is becoming more and more proactive on this issue area. However, even in the midst of all these initiatives, there are a number of policy analysts who ask that how India can take up emission reduction commitments in the midst of a range of issues such as poverty, livelihood protection, vulnerability and security. Taking into account all these aspects, how a climate change strategy can be calibrated is the main question before the environmentalists and policy analysts now.

Negotiations on the Road to Paris

In the 2014 Lima Conference itself, it was decided that countries would submit their INDCs to the UNFCCC before the starting of the COP-21 (Conference of Parties) at Paris. INDCs are the key instruments that give a detailed picture about how countries are planning to chalk out their emission reduction strategy for a post-2020 global climate change regime. Though INDCs are voluntary commitments, they are foundational to the framing of any agreement that intends to limit the global temperature below 2 degree Celsius from pre-industrial level. U.S., Russia and E.U. had announced their INDCs, much before the starting of the Paris summit. In the case of India, till September 2015 it had refrained from announcing its INDC target. One of the key reasons for this delay was out of the concern that whether these INDCs would be subjected to ex-ante review. India had maintained in the 2014 Lima Conference that, allowing INDCs for ex-ante review is completely objectionable as it can result in undermining the sovereignty of a state. Though the proposal for ex-ante review had to be dropped finally due to the widespread protests from various state actors, India's initial reluctance to announce its emission reduction plans pointing out this issue had given the image of a 'nay-sayer' for the country at the international level.

Equity issues have always taken the centre stage in climate change discussions. Before the starting of the Paris Conference, India had made it very clear that 'equity' must be central to the framing of any new agreement that replaces the Kyoto Protocol. India has always maintained that developed countries have benefited from past emissions of GHGs; so that, it is the responsibility of the developed industrialized states to reduce their GHG emissions, allowing the developing countries of the South which are lagging behind in the development ladder to focus more on their economic growth. India contends that highly industrialized countries like U.S. cannot move away from its ethical responsibility in polluting the atmosphere because U.S. has attained the current economic growth by emitting tonnes of GHGs into the atmosphere during the past many decades. U.S. is among the top national GHG emitters on per capita basis, and it comes second behind China in total tonnes of GHG emissions (World Resources Institute, 2011). As per the data collected by the CDIAC (Carbon Dioxide Information Analysis Centre), India's per capita CO_2 emissions is only 1.4 metric tonnes compared to that of the U.S.'s 17.22 metric tonnes (CDIAC, 2010).

Nevertheless, it is a fact that India cannot move away from taking up commitments for a long time in the context of its growing emissions. As a vulnerable country to the impacts of climate change, regulating emissions is in the national interest of India than any other developed country in the world. In India, majority of the emissions are from the elite sections, while rest of the population is reeling under severe poverty. It is expected that India's CO_2 emissions will at least triple in the next twenty years. The unprecedented growth of fossil-fuel based economies in India and China will increase the GHG emissions from these countries in the near future. During the negotiations prior to the Paris Conference, it was pointed out that the emissions from China and India are growing year by year; so that these two countries considering their current level of emissions and the potential for future emissions, must take up commitments under a new agreement. The pressure built by U.S. on India and China to announce their INDCs had also persuaded both the states to submit their INDCs to the UNFCCC before the starting of COP-21.

Issues related to the transfer of finance and technology to developing countries stood as another roadblock in the Paris negotiations. Majority of the developing countries have only less adaptive capacity to the effects of climate change. Small Island states are already facing the danger of sea level rise and thereby the threat of submergence. Majority of these states lack both financial and technological resources to combat the catastrophic effects of the crisis. In the past few years, much pressure was mounting on developed countries to extend financial and technological assistance to developing countries to enable them to fight against the challenge. However, not even half of the amount promised or technological help offered by these developed countries, have been delivered yet. The 2007 Bali Action Plan was instrumental in promising the transfer of finance and technology to the developing countries. It focused on three things: (i) mitigation of climate change, including measurable, reportable and verifiable national targets; (ii) enhanced action on adaptation, including financial needs, assessments and capacity-building; and (iii) enhanced action on technology development and transfer, and provision of financial resources and investment (UNFCCC, 2007).

Nevertheless, these commitments still remains unfulfilled. The Green Climate Fund which was given form at the Cancun Conference in 2010 with the objective to raise climate finance of US$ 100 billion a year by 2020 also failed in meeting its objective. One of the major concerns of developing countries before going to the Paris Conference was that how to conclude an agreement that enables the mobilization of financial and technological resources from developed countries.

Another driving factor that persuaded developing countries like India to submit its INDC was the very thought about the co-benefits of climate action. Climate change has larger implications on food security, water security, energy security and health security of any country. As one of the most vulnerable countries to the impacts of climate change, it is in the interest of India to adopt mechanisms to fight against this challenge. Taking up more concrete steps to address the climate crisis will bring substantial reduction in the overall emissions and will facilitate the ongoing national mission plans to achieve their intended objectives. It was in 2008 under the UPA Government, that India gave form to the National Action Plan on Climate Change (hereafter NAPCC).

Now, the policy of the current NDA government which is in power at the Centre has come under criticism as its climate policy is inconsistent with what it preaches at the international platforms. It is a paradox to find that, on the one hand Modi government advocates the use of solar energy and commits to increase the solar generated capacity to 100 gigawats, but on the other hand tries to double the production of coal which is a major source of carbon emission to meet the growing needs of the economy. On Teachers Day, in an interaction with the students, Prime Minister Modi had remarked that, "older people—70, 80 and 90 years old say in winter 'this time it is colder than last year'. Actually, it is not colder. People lose their ability to tolerate the cold as they grow older. In the same way, the climate has not changed. We have changed" (Is PM Modi a Climate Change Sceptic, 2014). This response had generated widespread criticism among the environmentalists, many labelling him as a climate sceptic and man of only rhetoric and not of action.

India's INDC Submission and Post-Paris Challenges

Climate change is a global problem, which needs to be addressed domestically and transnationally. It is important that collective responses need to be shaped to tackle the crisis at various levels. State actors have a decisive role in addressing the crisis. However, it is true that some of these actors try to deal with the issue from the prism of global domination and sometimes even as a tool to advance their self interests. In this context, finding a political solution to the climate crisis is increasingly difficult. Absence of consensus among major state actors regarding how to distribute the emission reduction burden among developing and developed country parties is making the decision-making process further complicated. It was after much consultations and deliberations finally, that the world countries agreed to submit their voluntary emission reduction pledges to the UNFCCC before the starting of the 2015 Paris Conference.

In the case of India, the most pertinent question is that, is it possible for India to achieve these stated objectives in its NDC document by taking into account its current developmental aspirations? In the midst of varied socio-economic issues, to what extent India would be able to balance between its developmental goals and emission reduction targets? If India has to achieve its stated objectives, at first it is important for the country to reduce its increasing dependence on fossil fuel based energy sources and switch over to renewable energy options.

Undoubtedly, climate change is a developmental as well environmental challenge for India. However, the emissions from developing countries like India are only 'survival' emissions, compared to that of the 'luxury' emissions from developed countries. Official statistics point out that "21 percent of Indians live on less than US$ 1.25 a day"

(Government of India, 2012). Moreover, India's per capita emissions is also too low compared to that of the per capita emissions from the developed countries. There are climate experts who argue that reducing emissions drastically in order to meet the INDC target would hamper the economic growth of the country adversely.

Agarwal and Narain (1991) argue that 'developed countries instead of paying up for their historical emissions, and asking developing countries to take up emission reduction burden is not justiciable. This is nothing else but 'environmental colonialism'. They reflect that 'the efforts of the developed countries to impose binding emission reduction targets upon developing countries which are less responsible for climate change is therefore unequal, unfair and imperialistic' (Agarwal and Narain, 1991). India's long standing demand to accommodate the principle of CBDR in the new agreement was out of all these concerns. The Paris agreement to a greater extent has succeeded in accommodating and acknowledging this CBDR principle.

Secondly, India's INDC promise of generating 40 percent of electric power capacity from non-fossil fuel sources would be a difficult task to carry out in the present context. At present, India is highly dependent upon coal and other fossil fuel based energy sources for its industrial and developmental activities. The emissions from India will continue to grow in the coming years if the country is reluctant to switch over to renewable energy sources. India has not fully utilized the potential of renewable energy sources such as wind energy, solar energy, nuclear energy and hydro power yet, to meet its growing energy needs.

These alternative energy sources are the most cost-effective energy sources that can help India to achieve its declared INDC target. Now, India is the 5th largest wind power player in the world. In terms of hydro power too, India has got vast potential to be explored. In terms of nuclear energy, India is still hesitant to use this cost-effective energy source. If India has to achieve the stated target of 40 percent electricity generation from non-fossil fuel sources, at first it should be receptive to initiate some concrete steps to explore the potential of these alternative energy sources.

Problems have been identified with India's National Action Plan on Climate Change too. The NAPCC has identified eight missions that include the National Solar Mission, National Mission for Sustainable Habitat, National Mission for Enhanced Energy Efficiency, National Water Mission, National Mission for Sustaining the Himalayan eco system, National Mission for a Green India, National Mission for Sustainable Agriculture and National Mission on Strategic Knowledge for Climate Change. Nevertheless, these missions have not brought any substantial progress in combating the challenge.

An evaluation study conducted by Byravan and Rajan (2012) based on the above mentioned eight national mission plans reveal that 'these missions remain as eight different blocks without setting any integrated target goal'. Apart from that, one important lacuna that has been identified with these missions is that it lacks clear-cut emission reduction targets. It fails to set up a time period to achieve its specified goals and objectives. Another important shortcoming of NAPCC is that 'the plan makes no attempt at all to reflect equity or redistributive principle. The only occasion of the mention of equity in the plan is when it deals with 'equity in per capita emissions' at the global level' (Byravan and Rajan, 2012).

Though NAPCC (2008) mentions about 'inclusive and sustainable development', it hasn't outlined any mechanisms so far to make these missions workable. In short, NAPCC lacks a long-term vision in its overall approach towards meeting India's stated target of reducing the emission intensity of its GDP from 33 percent to 35 percent by 2030 from the 2005 levels. Without sector specific emission reduction targets, achieving this ambitious INDC target seems to be less likely.

Another important promise in India's INDC document is that India would strive to create a carbon sink of 2.5 billion to

3 billion tonnes of CO_2 equivalent by expanding its forest cover (Government of India, 2015). However in the context of the gross violations of various environmental laws including that of Forest Rights Act, Water and Air Pollution Act, Environmental Protection Act and Wildlife Protection Act, achieving this target seems to be difficult. Recently, the Ministry of Environment, Forest and Climate Change, had intervened in order to bring some amendments to the environmental impact assessment rules and to the Forest Rights Act. Environmentalists point out that these proposed amendments would only help to dilute the existing environmental laws of the country and thereby leading to further environmental destruction and deforestation. As many argue, it is important for the Government to focus on achieving higher economic growth.

However, if the state fails to address the environmental concerns, it will lead to an uneven development path. There is nothing wrong in focusing on economic growth and attracting more investments to the country. However, the most important question is whether the growth achieved by completely destroying the environment and eco-system is sustainable? Development does not mean selling off land, sand and water to the non-state actors. If development is not inclusive, sustainable and equitable it won't help India in any way to materialise its INDC commitments including that of expansion of the forest cover.

India has always maintained that CBDR principle and respective capability (RC) of countries should be important constituents in the framing of a new climate change regime. As national circumstances of the countries are different and their issues are varied, one cannot assume that almost all countries would be on an equal footing to combat this challenge. Financially and technologically, these developing countries are not well equipped yet to fight against this global menace. In this context, demanding these countries to strictly comply with their INDC targets without transferring them adequate financial and technological resources would only undermine the efforts to reinstate equity in the climate regime. Therefore, due consideration to the countries' 'respective capability', should remain as a top priority while giving form to a new climate regime.

It is true that India's recent INDC pledges have helped the country to shed its nay-sayer image and project itself as a climate pro-activist at the international level. India's INDC submission was a surprise to many developed countries as it was for the first time that India submitted some concrete action plans to combat the challenge. India's INDC pledges are fair and ambitious compared to the emission reduction pledges submitted by many developed countries including that of the U.S. Nevertheless, it is a crucial question that how India would achieve the stated objectives in the INDC, in the context of ever growing emissions.

On the one hand, Government is initiating new steps to explore the potential of renewable energy sources to keep the emissions under control; but on the other hand, the Government is lethargic in its efforts to cut down India's increasing dependence on coal and other fossil fuel based energy sources. Many have already pointed out that for India, INDC pledges are difficult to fulfil as it is inconsistent with its domestic action plans.

If India has to meet its INDC pledges, it is important for the country to give form to sector specific emission reduction plans in its NAPCC initiative. Moreover, fulfilment of India's INDC commitments is partially dependent upon the transfer of financial and technological resources from outside too. As it is the case, only if various factors come in favour of India, the country would be able to fulfil its declared INDC target. In the present context, meeting this target seems to be less likely.

References

Agarwal, Anil and Narain, Sunita (1991), "Global Warming in an Unequal World: A Case of Environmental Colonialism", Centre for Science and Environment, New Delhi.

Byravan S, Rajan, Chella (2012), "Sea Level Rise: Impact on Major Infrastructure, Ecosystems and Land along the Tamil Nadu Coast", in Dubash N.K. (ed.), 'Handbook of Climate Change and India: Development, Politics and Governance', New Delhi: Oxford University Press.

Carbon Dioxide Information Analysis Centre (CDIAC) (2010), "Carbon Dioxide Emissions, Metric Tons of CO_2 Per Capita", Oak Ridge National Library, Oak Ridge: Tennessee, available at: http://data.un.org/Data.aspx?d=MDG&f=seriesRow ID:751.

Gandhi, Indira (1972), "Man and Environment", address to the Plenary Session of the United Nations Conference on the Human Environment, Stockholm, 14 June, available at: http://www.unlibrarynairobi.org/PDFs/Only_one_earth.pdf.

Government of India (2008), "National Action Plan on Climate Change: Prime Minister's Council on Climate Change", available at: http://pmindia.nic.in/climate_change.htm.

Government of India (2012), "Brief on Climate Finance", Ministry of Finance, New Delhi.

Government of India (2015), "India's Intended Nationally Determined Contribution", Ministry of Environment, Forest and Climate Change, New Delhi.

"Is PM Modi A Climate Change Sceptic?" *The Citizen*, New Delhi, September 26, 2014.

Ki-moon, Ban (2007), "Climate Change Poses Defining Challenge of Our Time, Ban Says", lecture delivered on November 17 at the U.N Headquarters, New York, available at: http://www.un.org/apps/news/story.asp?NewsID=28458#.U2CJsFWSycg.

PTI (2010), "Don't Read Too Much into Jairam Ramesh's Statement at Cancun: PM", *The Times of India,* available at: http://articles.timesofindia.indiatimes.com/2010-12-10/india/28256891_1_binding-commitments-climate-changejairam-ramesh.

Sarkar, Dipankar De (2009), "Slated at Home, Jairam Ramesh Is Praised by US, Britain", *Hindustan Times*, October 20, 2009.

United Nations Framework Convention on Climate Change (2007), "Report of the Conference of the Parties on its Thirteenth Session", held in Bali from December 3 to 15, 2007", Bali: United Nations, available at:

http://unfccc.int/ resource/docs/2007/cop13/eng/06a01.pdf.

World Commission on Environment and Development (1987), "Our Common Future", Oxford: Oxford University Press.

World Resources Institute (2011), "Country GHG Emissions", Washington, D.C.

9

India's Act East Policy

Rajiv Bhatia

Introduction

East Asia, the vast region stretching from Myanmar to Japan, Australia and the Pacific Island States, is now one of the most important theatres of world politics and economy. This region, together with India, has been the beneficiary of a gradual shift of power and economic growth from the west to the east. Developments within it will determine whether the 21st century turns out to be 'Asia's century', one that is marked by peace, security and development for all or by an era of untrammelled rivalry, disputes, tensions and conflict.

After South Asia and Major Powers, this region has been the principal object of New Delhi's political and diplomatic attention and action in recent years. Since the formation of the Modi government in May 2014, the trend gathered further momentum. During the past nearly two years, India's president, vice president and prime minister visited nine out of ten member-states of the ASEAN. The president is also likely to visit the 10th country—the Philippines—before the end of 2016. In addition, Prime Minister Narendra Modi paid visits to China, Japan, Australia, South Korea, Mongolia and Fiji. Besides, there has been a long series of high-level visits from this region to India. President Barack Obama's visit to India in January 2015 was also highly relevant in this context. All these visits and interactions witnessed a marked evolution of India-East Asia relations through comprehensive dialogues and conclusion of numerous important agreements.

Stakes in the Indo-Pacific or Asia-Pacific or East Asian region are huge. The situation is complex and in a flux. Future developments will be moulded by an intricate interplay of economy, politics, defence and diplomacy of key stakeholders such as US, China, India, Japan, ASEAN and others. Hence, the larger regional and global context needs to be kept in view as we examine the trajectory and impact of India's policy towards the East.

From Look East Policy (LEP) to Act East Policy (AEP)

Most scholars trace the birth or origin of India's Look East Policy (LEP) to the early 1990s when P.V. Narasimha Rao was the prime minister. India was facing a grave economic situation and needed to attract capital and technological cooperation from the successful ASEAN economies. Following the end of the Cold War that had resulted in the triumph of the US and extinction of the Soviet Union, India found itself 'friend-less'; consequently, it embarked on a search for new friendships and partnerships. Insurgencies in the North-east also compelled the central government to seek cooperation of the eastern neighbours, especially Myanmar, to bring about peace and security.

On its part, ASEAN too sought India's engagement as a way to balance China and other powers so that Southeast Asia continued to be a region of peace and prosperity. India's vast market was also an important attraction. A mix of these circumstances and motivations drove India and ASEAN to initiate a dialogue partnership in 1992, which moved from sectoral dialogue, through full dialogue, to the summit-level dialogue in 2002. In the year 2017, the two sides will celebrate the silver anniversary of their dialogue partnership and 15 years of the summit-level relationship.

Tracing the development of LEP, Amar Nath Ram points out that, in its first phase (1992-2002), the policy was largely confined to trade and economic relations with ASEAN, whereas, in its second phase (2002-12), it saw 'consolidation and expansion' of India's links with the region 'to now encompass, among others, political, strategic, defence, economic, science and technology and cultural areas of cooperation'. [1]

Public memory is proverbially short, but scholars cannot be accused of amnesia. They are always conscious of history, ready to draw suitable lessons from it. Hence, S.D. Muni is right in arguing that the policy has 'a strong historical legacy' and pointing out that '...the Look East Policy did not come just from nowhere in 1991'. [2] Two points are noteworthy here. First, India's extensive exchanges and linkages with the eastern countries should be viewed as *four waves*—pre-colonial, colonial, post-Independence and since 1990—as advised by this eminent scholar. Secondly, the origin of Prime Minister Narasimha Rao's 'Look East Policy' (LEP) could be traced to the diplomatic initiatives his predecessor, Prime Minister Rajiv Gandhi, took in the mid-1980s. Yet, it is also necessary to recognize that specific and powerful factors appeared in the early 1990s in India (and its North-east), ASEAN and the larger region, which led to the birth and development of LEP.

In this context, readers may be advised to peruse two valuable books on the subject, both edited by Amar Nath Ram and published at the initiative of the Indian Council of World Affairs (ICWA). These are: *Two Decades of India's Look East Policy* and *India's Asia-Pacific Engagement*.

A little known fact also deserves to be mentioned here. Before the Act East Policy (AEP) acquired wide usage, Paramjit S. Sahai, a former high commissioner to Malaysia, wrote, 'India would have also to give a new thrust to its LEP. I would like to call it 'Act East Policy', while some of my friends from ASEAN would like to call it 'Go East Policy'. [3]

Prime Minister Narendra Modi specifically mentioned the transformation of Look East Policy into Act East Policy at the India-ASEAN Summit in Naypyitaw in November 2014. Before him, the phrase 'Act East Policy' was used by External Affairs Minister Sushma Swaraj. Analysts also refer to the fact that, while obliquely criticizing LEP, US Secretary of State

Hillary Clinton had advised India to not only 'look east' but also 'act east'.

What is the Difference?

Critics of the Modi government's Act East Policy seem to suggest that there is little difference between this policy and LEP. Others tend to emphasize the novelty and originality of AEP. The fact of the matter is that AEP is a conscious upgradation of LEP, a calibrated response to the changing situation in the region as well as to the evolution of India's priorities in its economic and security strategies.

As this author has argued elsewhere, [1] a careful comparison of LEP and AEP shows that the new edition of the previous policy has five notable features:

Firstly, the focus on tangible action and concrete results is inherent in the change from 'Look' to 'Act'.

Secondly, while ASEAN continues to be the central pillar or core of the policy, South Block is investing much more (than before) in deepening cooperation with the extended region, comprising in particular US, Japan, Australia and South Korea, in order to cope with a marked increase in China's assertiveness.

Consequently, the third feature is boldness on India's part in the security, defence and strategic domain.

Fourthly, India might become even more cordial and cooperative with ASEAN, but hard-nosed too. At the first summit itself, the Indian PM called for conducting 'a review of our free trade agreement'. A strong push is being given to negotiations for the Regional Comprehensive Economic Partnership (RCEP) with the aim to conclude them in 2016. Besides, higher dedication was promised for creating 'the trident' of commerce, culture and connectivity.

Finally, the new government indicated clearly that India's North Eastern Region (NER) would receive a higher priority in the implementation of AEP.

Present Status of Relationships

In this section, one may evaluate briefly the two main components of AEP, namely: (i) India's relations with ASEAN, and (ii) relations with the extended region comprising the non-ASEAN states. That one impacts the other and both help us to form a holistic view, is quite evident. The significant point is that AEP now deals with the entire region, and it pertains to economic, political, security and strategic aspects of cooperation with all the principle players in East Asia.

ASEAN: Since the launch of LEP in the early 1990s, the multifaceted partnership between India and ASEAN has come a long way. As Prime Minister Manmohan Singh observed at the historic summit in December 2012:

"The breadth and intensity of India's engagement with Southeast Asia is unmatched by any of our other regional relationships". [5]

The Vision Statement issued at the ASEAN-India Commemorative Summit in December 2012 reflected several new trends in the relationship. Two of them need special mention here, namely: (i) ASEAN's appreciation of 'India's commitment to continue the special focus on the CLMV countries that represents a bridge between ASEAN and India through human resource development and capacity building, and (ii) the joint commitment to enhance connectivity through various measures. [6]

At the beginning of 2016, the strategic partnership between India and ASEAN appeared to be in good shape, even though its full potential awaits realization. This is confirmed by the following developments.

1. India has welcomed and supported the creation of the ASEAN Community in December 2015 (the work is still in progress). External Affairs Minister Sushma Swaraj observed: ASEAN's achievements over the last five decades have been truly impressive, especially considering the diversity of challenges that it has been confronted with, both internally and externally. [7] ASEAN has been deeply

appreciative of the Modi government's new policy initiatives at home and abroad. New Delhi believes that 'in this difficult moment, India and ASEAN are two bright spots of optimism'. [8]

2. Two summits (in 2014 and 2015) produced substantive outcomes. Thirty annual dialogue mechanisms are in existence. Three funds, namely ASEAN-India Cooperation Fund, Science and Technology Fund and Green Fund are in operation to finance a variety of projects. The S&T Fund has been enhanced from US$ 1 million to US$ 5 million. Action Plan for 2016-20 has been adopted in August 2015. Cooperation encompasses diverse sectors such as trade and investment, food, agriculture, tourism and ICT etc.
3. Unlike some other nations, India adheres to the principle of 'the centrality of ASEAN' in East Asian affairs. 'The centrality of ASEAN has become the fulcrum, around which the Asia-Pacific region has evolved and its importance has increased further in recent times'. [9] It is hoped that ASEAN will appreciate the need for its own unity, solidarity and integration as the fundamental basis on which this centrality is clearly dependent.
4. India is taking the question of security, including maritime security (both against traditional and non-traditional variety), with utmost seriousness. Its views on the situation in the South China Sea have been articulated frequently with clarity and consistency. The essence is a call for 'restraint', 'responsibility', adherence to international law and norms, upholding of freedom of navigation and security of sea-lanes and, above all, avoiding the threat or use of force. ASEAN has reason to be assured of India's continuing support for an early conclusion of negotiations for a binding Code of Conduct (CoC), building up on the previous Declaration on Code of Conduct (DOC).
5. India advocates an inclusive, balanced, transparent and open regional architecture for security and cooperation in the Asia-Pacific. ASEAN-India consultations and cooperation are

getting deepened through various ASEAN-led fora, including the East Asia Summit, ASEAN Defence Ministers' Meeting and expanded ASEAN Maritime Forum.

6. The Modi government has announced two new initiatives: (a) a Project Development Fund with a substantial corpus of ₹ 500 crore (about US$ 75 million) to develop manufacturing hubs in CLMV countries, and (b) a new Line of Credit of US$ 1 billion to promote projects that support physical and digital connectivity between India and ASEAN. Vice President Hamid Ansari, while speaking at Chulalongkorn University on February 4, 2016, observed: 'The rationale for a strong ASEAN-India Strategic Partnership is clearer than ever'. It is, therefore, 'natural' that the two sides would work 'towards a qualitatively more substantive and invigorated relationship'. [10]

Extended Region: With regard to the extended region covering non-ASEAN countries, it may first be useful to pinpoint the key trends reflected in main developments during the current decade. Territorial disputes between China and a few countries in the South China Sea and the East China Sea, the arms' build-up, the unspoken competition between two emerging economic groupings like TPP and RCEP, debate on a new regional security architecture, and on cooperation to counter non-traditional threats to security, and China's drive towards 'One Belt, One Road' (OBOR) and 'Maritime Silk Route' (MSR) initiatives—all combine to reflect the current concerns and priorities. Evidently, the Indo-Pacific landscape has been undergoing, as scholar-diplomat A.N. Ram put it aptly, a reconfiguration of the tenuous post-Cold War political equilibrium, strategic balance, military and maritime positioning and economic expansion and competition.

What these trends reflect, in their essence, is a strategic contestation between the US—the dominant power—and China—the rising power—for re-ordering of their roles in the Asia-Pacific region. Scholars, recalling similar conflicts of the past between Sparta and Athens, Great Britain and Germany, the US and the USSR, caution that a purely binary approach to define the ongoing US-China rivalry should be eschewed. They point to its unusual complexity, given the two nations' intense mutual economic inter-dependence as well as the apparent desire of regional players to continue profiting from China's economic rise even as some of them experience strategic discomfort and anxiety over China's behaviour. Prevailing uncertainties have led experts to argue that the region has to prepare itself for divergent outcomes: sharpening of competition, expansion of cooperation, and possibility of confrontation and conflict.

In this light, the Modi government pursues a policy that blends India's economic, political and strategic imperatives. The focus is on accelerating economic growth, connectivity with ASEAN and beyond, and maritime security. At the same time, there is evidence of calibrated boldness on strategic issues. This is reflected in endeavours to improve relations with China, while taking the strategic partnerships with US, Japan, Australia and South Korea to a new level of consolidation as evident from the new agreements signed in the past two years and several other actions.

Policies designed to strengthen India's defence capabilities would be followed with vigour, but basic fault lines would be maintained. This explains New Delhi's call for the region to concentrate on economic development and avoid tensions and conflict. A significant element of this policy is to help the East Asia Summit (EAS) to be strengthened and made more effective. This last point needs some elaboration here. In our view, EAS should be rejuvenated and enabled to emerge as a cross between the UN Security Council and G-20 Summit. [11]

A generally neglected component of AEP is India's engagement with the Pacific Island Developing Countries (PIDC), which has been on a steady increase. It should be viewed as 'an extension' of LEP and AEP. In a useful essay, Bhaskar Balakrishnan has argued that while 'relations with Fiji have developed well keeping in view special factors, India's relations with the other Pacific Island countries offer much scope for further expansion'. [12] His conclusion—that 'there is a requirement for strengthening India's capacity for interacting effectively with this region'—deserves close attention. [13]

A brief reference to the concept of 'Indo-Pacific' region is inescapable here. It is essentially a geopolitical construct, conveying the deep interlinkage of security-development paradigm in the Indian and Pacific oceans, with India occupying a pivotal position in the strategic calculus. The term has gained acceptance among policymakers in India and elsewhere, but is opposed by Chinese scholars and officials. As Shankari Sundaraman argues, 'the scope and depth of India's interaction' with the region 'needs to be substantially enhanced which will critically test India's abilities in the future'. She stresses that, in the context of US-China rivalry, 'India's embrace of the Indo-Pacific will certainly be more strategic than semantic'. [14]

Sanjeev Bhaduria views the Pacific in the specific context of unfolding power rivalries. His argument is, "India's foreign policy in the Pacific is now aimed at curtailing the influence of China and establish itself as a major player. Towards this end, it has taken the help of the US and Japan with whom it shares many values and interests in the region. [15]

Shashi Tharoor highlights the possibility of India having 'an intriguing role' in the context of 'the global contention for power and global influence between the United States and India'. [16]

Looking at prospects of the next decade, Yogendra Kumar has suggested that India would need to strengthen its relations with ASEAN, while diminishing its focus on grouping's institutions, given their limitations. His view is that India would be compelled 'to explore other options and follow a differentiated policy towards the ASEAN member countries'. [17]

Conclusion

In December 2016 when the Modi government reaches the mid-point of its five-year term, we may be in a sound position to judge the results of the AEP. A five-point yardstick, as articulated by this author elsewhere [18] and delineated below, may be useful for the proposed evaluation:

1. Trade ($77 billion in 2014-15) and investment ($71 billion during 2007-15) between India and ASEAN need to increase. Without this, AEP may be unable to claim spectacular success in the future.
2. India-ASEAN connectivity projects, started long ago, need to be completed at the earliest. Deadlines for completion of the Kaladan multi-modal transport project in Myanmar and the trilateral highway project (linking India, Myanmar and Thailand) are 2019 and 2018 respectively. New Delhi has to do everything possible to avoid further slippages. The two new initiatives mentioned above—for CLMV and for ASEAN—should also be put into effect as soon as possible.
3. Considering that the Trans Pacific Partnership (TPP) is heading towards fruition, parties to the negotiations for RCEP pact (i.e. ASEAN, India and others) can hardly afford further delay in finalizing and signing it. The common objective is to complete this task before the end of 2016. Will this be achieved?
4. Countries concerned about the situation relating to the South China Sea might just succeed in persuading China not to rock the boat too much. Military conflict or accidents have to be avoided, even if political tensions and arms race might continue. This will bear a close watch.
5. Finally, elevation of the East Asia Summit (EAS) into an effective platform for policy coordination would be another important facet to watch.

In the end, one may add that the internal dimensions of AEP, [19] relating to our North-eastern region, are also very important. Tangible progress in enhancing connectivity within this region will need to be ensured in the coming years.

Endnotes

1. Amar Nath Ram (ed.) (2015), "India's Asia-Pacific Engagement: Impulses and Imperatives", New Delhi: Manohar, pp. 23-25.
2. S.D. Muni (2012), "Look East Policy: Beyond Myths", in A.N. Ram (ed.), 'Two Decades of India's Look East Policy: Partnership for Peace, Progress and Prosperity', New Delhi: Manohar, p. 205.
3. Paramjit S. Sahai (2012), "India-ASEAN: Thirsting for a New Thrust, Relationship", in A.N. Ram (ed.), "Two Decades of India's Look East Policy: Partnership for Peace, Progress and Prosperity", New Delhi: Manohar, p. 120.
4. Rajiv Bhatia, "India's Act East Policy and Myanmar's Role", distinguished lecture series, Ministry of External Affairs, March 10, 2016, available at: http://www.mea.gov.in/distinguished-lectures-detail.htm?464.
5. Opening statement by Prime Minister at Plenary Session of India-ASEAN Commemorative Summit, December 20, 2012, Ministry of External Affairs, New Delhi, available at: http://www.mea.gov.in/Speeches-Statements.htm?dtl/20981/Opening_Statement_by_Prime_Minister_at_Plenary_Session_of_IndiaASEAN_Commemorative_Summit.
6. Vision Statement-ASEAN-India Commemorative Summit, December 20, 2012, Ministry of External Affairs, New Delhi, available at: http://www.mea.gov.in/bilateral-documents.htm?dtl/20982/Vision_StatementASEANIndia_Commemorative_Summit.
7. Keynote Address by External Affairs Minister at the Ministerial Session of Delhi Dialogue VIII, February 18, 2016, available at: http://www.mea.gov.in/Speeches-Statements.htm?dtl/26367/Keynote_Address_by_External_Affairs_Minister_at_the_Ministerial_Session_of_Delhi_Dialogue_VIII_February_18_2016.
8. Opening statement by Prime Minister at 13th ASEAN-India Summit in Kuala Lumpur, (November 21, 2015.
9. Keynote Address by External Affairs Minister at the Ministerial Session of Delhi Dialogue VIII, February 18, 2016, available at: http://www.mea.gov.in/Speeches-

Statements.htm?dtl/26367/Keynote_Address_by_External_Affairs_Minister_at_the_Ministerial_Session_of_Delhi_Dialogue_VIII_February_18_2016.

10. Address by Shri M. Hamid Ansari, Hon'ble Vice President of India at Chulalongkorn University, Bangkok, February 4, 2016, available at: http://vicepresidentofindia.nic.in/contents.asp?id=574.
11. Rajiv K. Bhatia (2015), "India in Global Affairs", New Delhi: KW Publishers. For the author's views on this and other related suggestions, please see pages 58-59.
12. B. Balakrishnan, "India's Engagement with the Pacific Islands", *Indian Foreign Affairs Journal*, Volume 10, No. 4, October-December, 2015, p. 353.
13. Ibid., p. 365.
14. Shankari Sundaraman (2015), "India and the Indo-Pacific: Semantic Change or Strategic Shift", in Gauri Khandekar (ed.), 'The EU-India Strategic Partnership: Facing the Foreign Policy Divide', New Delhi: Lenin Media, p. 138.
15. Sanjeev Bhaduria (2016), "Emerging India in the Asia Pacific", in Kousar J. Azam (ed.), 'India in World Affairs: The Next Decade', Delhi: Manohar, p. 439.
16. Shashi Tharoor (2012), "Pax Indica: India and the World of the 21st Century", New Delhi: Allen Lane, Penguin Group, p. 146. His full argument is: 'And yet, in the context of the global contention for power and global influence between the United States and China, India may well have an intriguing role: the increasing Indo-US closeness could actually serve to make improving relations with India a higher priority for China than it might otherwise have been, by reminding China of India's potential to serve US interests, perhaps to China's detriment'.
17. Yogendra Kumar (2015), "India-ASEAN Relations: The Next Ten Years", in Surendra Kumar (ed.), 'India and the World: Through the Eyes of Indian Diplomats', New Delhi: Wisdom Tree, p. 230.
18. Rajiv Bhatia, "India's Act East Policy and Myanmar's Role", distinguished lecture series, Ministry of External Affairs (March 10, 2016, available at: http://www.mea.gov.in/distinguished-lectures-detail.htm?464. Please also see, "Act East Policy: Emerging Contours", January 13, 2016, available at:

http://www.orfonline.org/research/act-east-policy-emerging-contours-2.

19. Rajiv K. Bhatia (2015), "India in Global Affairs: Perspectives from Sapru House", New Delhi: KW Publishers. Please see the chapter entitled, 'ASEAN-India: Shaping the Post-2015 Agenda'.

Index

Index